Across The Clouds

Daniele Schmechel

ISBN 978-0-692-52173-1
Library of Congress Control Number 2015914247

First Edition 2015

Dedication

I dedicate this book to my life-companion, Don, to my children, Chris, Stefanie, and Heidi and to my grandchildren, Charlotte, Elliott, Sophie, Zoe, Julian, and Mia.

May this book help them understand a little bit better their French wife, mother and grandmother!

Contents

Foreword

On November 23, 1964, I met Daniele at a "Thanksgiving party" in cold and wintry Grenoble. From across the room, I was attracted to the strong, natural leader that had organized this party for American students. I soon fell in love with her and have spent my entire life with this marvelous and challenging woman.

She is amazingly stubborn, brilliant, analytical and sassy. She attributes her strong character to her combined Norman and Basque ancestry and heritage. A distinguished line of female relatives have served in the Ursuline religious order.

Over the last year, Daniele has carefully crafted an epic collection of word stories and pictures of her life's journey. These writings are very French in style and manner, yet in beautiful and poetic English. The book is not an autobiography, not a Christian book, not a "Grandmother" book for grandchildren, but rather a passionate and moving epic memoire of one woman's life. Written in lyrical style, I have read each chapter over the last year, one by one, as they were slowly handcrafted. Some words and passages have moved me to the "tears of fire" spoken of by the Desert Fathers of old. As I have read other pages, I have just as often broken out in laughter by her French analysis and reactions to a new land, a new people and American life and religion.

I have visited all of the sacred places of her youth that are mentioned in these pages. Since God joined us together in 1964, I have witnessed all the events, dreams, and trials of our life together.. I am not a person of visions and dreams, but my wife does experience this side of God's light and majesty. As a neurologist and person of Christian faith, I bear scientific witness to the amazing ability of the human mind and spirit to respond to our Creator, His Light and His voice. I bear further personal witness to the prayers, events and miracles spoken of in these pages.

My choice of a career as an academic neuroscientist and practicing neurologist forms part of the background of our life as a couple and family. My love of science, research and medical practice consumed much energy and time. My long hours and times away from my family are now a somewhat bitter memory, but are now behind me. Watching the birth and creation of "Across the Clouds" has led to healing of memories for me and a vital understanding of the gracious miracles, interventions, patience and forgiveness that preserved our hearts and marriage over these many years.

I release you the reader to a unique experience that will transform you.

Donald E Schmechel, MD

ONE

August 1942

Many times have I heard this story!
Many times have I questioned its validity!

Did it really happen as my father said or were his words the product of a fertile imagination?

I remember it as if it were yesterday for how can one forget such an incredible and almost magical tale...

I remember it as if I was still the little girl listening to her dad's gentle voice. I often did not know if I was supposed to be happy, sad or afraid! For this story had not been conceived and birthed in an imaginary world filled with fairies and handmaidens where most characters sooner or later, would live happily ever after. My bedtime story had been birthed in a land filled with darkness, destruction and death and yet, to the eyes of a little girl, it was a happy story for it had a good ending! I was told, night after night, that God had reached across the clouds to save my life. I was reminded, night after night, how special I was and how much God loved me.

The time was August 1942 and I was one month old, oblivious to the inconceivable tragedy that was spreading across the entire world, one city at a time, one country at a time! I was born in Versailles, France but my parents and I lived in Paris where, much later, I was told that thousands of homes and apartment buildings had been ripped apart and blown to pieces by nightly air raids and where thousands of lives had been lost in the never-ending carnage. It was also in August 1942, that thousands of French Jewish children had been shipped to concentration camps where they had all perished in airless gas chambers.

On that particular night, my father had taken my mother and I to an underground shelter for as always, the dreaded sirens had announced an approaching air raid. The bombs had kept on falling around us, destroying lives and destroying buildings, including our house, which had evaporated in a split second!

I still remember seeing sadness in my father's eye as he told this story! And yet, he would keep on going, keep on speaking for he always looked forward to its happy ending. He looked forward to the moment when he would be able to say that I, the heroine of his story, had lived happily ever after!

One single bomb had rendered us homeless but for the time being, on that particular night, we were in an underground shelter, fearing the worst. The explosions kept on getting closer and closer and the bombs kept on falling...

My father knew that there was no way we would be able to survive these relentless attacks and he was so frightened that he could physically hear his entire body shake, bone against bone, knuckle against knuckle! And yet, because he was my dad, he was holding me as tight as he could, trying to protect me with his very own life as if he could!

He then heard another bomb falling from the sky and somehow, knew that it was the one that would hit us and kill us all! He knew that the underground shelter would not be strong enough to shield us from a certain death if this particular bomb exploded! It did land on top of the shelter, but it did not explode!

Still holding me as tight as he could and still shaking as much as ever, he walked outside a few minutes later and stared in silence and wonder at the bomb, which was lying on the ground, a few feet from him.

It had been designed to kill us but somehow, had been unable to detonate!

As I grew older, it was hard to understand and rationalize why my life had been spared when so many people had lost theirs?

And yet, there was no doubt in my mind and my heart that my life as well as the lives of my parents and the few people who had shared this fateful underground shelter had been preserved miraculously, on a fateful night, in August 1942. I wish I had had the chance to meet them, to see their faces and to know their lives. Were they aware that they had been given a miraculous second chance? Did it lead them to God or did they choose to forget that it had ever happened…?

We were saved but what about the thousands who had perished and the others who would lose their lives in the next three years? Why had I been chosen to survive? Why had my life been spared? Why was a one-month-old baby girl given a second chance…?

I do not have the answer to the questions above but I know that one-day, God will open the book of life, the book of my life and help me understand the whys.

I was, after all, not the only one who had survived this attack and yet, my father made me feel, throughout my childhood, as if I had been the only one!

My father kept on reminding me how special I was and how much God loved me!

It was much more than a bedtime story! It was a magical tale from high above that, night after night, formed my character and planted in my young heart, the absolute assurance that God had loved me enough to save my life!

My father's daily affirmations had a life-long effect on my destiny for I was made to feel special and it helped me understand, even at a young age, that God was watching over me! And yet, I cannot but ask why He was not watching over the millions who perished during the Second World War?

I was one of twenty some people whose lives had been spared and I wonder if each and everyone understood the magnificent gift that they had received on that night... I wonder if they ever realized that their lives were no longer their own...

Since our house was gone, we left Paris and lived in the countryside, near Switzerland where food was plentiful and where one could lead an almost normal life in the midst of an abnormal world! We stayed there until the end of the war and although we had lost our house, we still had plenty. The war may have been raging outside the area where we lived but as far as I was concerned, life was wonderful!

I was very young but my memory is as clear as a bell for I remember playing in the snow with the baker's children who lived across the road from our new house. Life was as good as it could be as I helped our landlord tend to her horses, feed her chickens and pick her green beans and juicy tomatoes! I was a happy little girl, tended to by her nanny, oblivious to the fact that there was and had been a war and yet, beginning to realize that things were not as good as they could be on my home front! For my parents fought quite a bit with each other and my mother seemed to be "different" from everyone else!

A year or two after the war was over, we settled down in Versailles where my grandparents lived and where everyone tried to lead a life as normal as possible in the midst of an abnormal world and an adverse outside environment! I was, once again, sheltered for food was always plentiful and I lived in a beautiful house surrounded by an even more beautiful park!

My grandparents were not only wealthy but also very strict when it came to the upbringing of their grandchildren and they made sure, not only then but also throughout the remainder of their lives that I would be raised as a proper young lady and bring honor to their names and their noble heritage! I loved them dearly and they had a lasting influence on my life!

I had not only survived the war, I had also survived its aftermath and as my father embarked on a new career, we moved to Clermont-Ferrand where I was soon enrolled in an elite boarding school.

As I said earlier, writing this chapter was far from easy and my only escape is to be as honest as I can be with the hope that you will understand why I still do not have all the answers to the many "whys" that pertain to these moments and these days.

As I said earlier, neither was I special nor am I special...!

On that fateful night, I was simply a one-month-old little French baby girl who was totally oblivious to what had just happened and yet, whose life was preserved by a supernatural and sovereign move of God's hand!

TWO

Ursuline Convent

As I said, in the previous chapter, my parents moved shortly after the war ended, to Clermont Ferrand, which was located smack in the middle of the Auvergne Mountains. It was a land of extinct volcanoes, beautiful medieval villages and ruins of long ago. It was a land where ghosts and fairy tales abounded and where wolves could still be found roaming at night.

Located in Clermont-Ferrand was the most elite boarding school in all of France, which my grandparents as well as my parents had decided I would be attending. Saint Alyre was run by Ursuline nuns and consisted of a large school as well as a convent.

Although I had to wear a dreaded uniform and had to learn to curtsy, I liked being there! The convent was centuries old, large and very beautiful, surrounded by parks and forests, which I loved to explore during recess time. Having been born with a fertile imagination, I often, would imagine myself back in the magical time of knights and fair maidens.

I was daily being taught and trained to be a proper young lady, proficient in many scholarly subjects, fluent in several languages and totally oblivious to the outside world! My parents travelled quite often and for this reason, my school soon became my second home! But I did not like being boarded on weekends and I abhorred the cold showers that I had to take every morning at dawn. I liked even less eating horsemeat every day of the week except for dreaded codfish on Fridays! But I made many friends and life soon settled to a routine.

From the outside, everything looked wonderful for I was living a very sheltered life in the midst of post war France!

My nanny was like a mother to me and I was never allowed to be alone when being outside for she walked me to school every day, and escorted me to my weekly classes at the Opera House where I was studying ballet. I do not ever remember playing outside as I observed other children doing. Many of my friends lived in manors or estates and these were my playgrounds! For we were all carrying pedigrees and we were all expected to behave a certain way, to always be proper and polite and to never play in the mud...!

My parents lived in a beautiful and large apartment and I do not remember my mother ever spending time in the kitchen, cleaning or doing laundry! This kind of work was relegated to the servants and the cook whom I adored. Knowing my dislike of horsemeat and codfish, they made sure that I was always well fed and happy. I adored their fried "beignets" dipped in powdered sugar and their scrumptious Sunday dinners. Although I was never shown nor taught to cook, it was then and there that I developed a passion for French cooking!

I loved going to church on Sunday mornings. The music, the Latin Mass as well as the incense and the light coming from countless candles transported me into a world of my own. This was a world to which I retreated with a mixture of excitement and wonder. It was then and there that I began to love God, Jesus and the Holy Spirit although I was far too young to understand it all!

As you probably guessed by now, I was raised in a very formal environment. My paternal grandfather was still the president of a large bank in Paris. If his children had been driven to school every morning by the family chauffeur, he made sure that my nanny never left me walk to school alone! My grandmother came from an aristocratic family where lords and knights from long ago had fought and conquered many battles. She also made sure that I would be properly raised and at times, she felt more like a hawk than a grandmother and yet, I knew that she loved me dearly! They both were fully aware of the volatile home environment in which I was being raised and thus, had chosen to watch over me and be intimately involved in my upbringing. For this and for their love, I will be eternally grateful.

My father had never been allowed nor taught to express love while growing up and I do not ever remember him saying the words, that as a child, I needed to hear. I never heard him say, "I love you" and yet, I am sure that he loved me as best as he knew how!

My mother, on the other hand, was kind of "unusual." I knew from an early age that she was different from the rest of the world! She could be sweet and loving one moment and turn into an absolute terror the next moment. Her rages were never directed toward me for I was almost constantly under the protection of my nanny or my grandparents. But she was extremely suspicious of everyone and seemed to always direct her anger toward my father, accusing him of improprieties that had been most certainly birthed into her twisted mind. His business papers would often end up being thrashed across the floor and our furniture seemed always to be found upturned! I would then run to my bedroom, lock the door and try to deafen her dreaded screams by covering my ears. My room may have been beautiful and filled with exquisite antiques but it had now become my prison. My safe places were my convent, my church and my God!

The war outside may have ended but the war, within my house, was raging every night, creating havoc on my emotions and my heart.

As a result, I started to stutter and I was soon unable to utter a host of words. From being a "bright" child,

I became a "handicapped" child! I was no longer popular in school for who wants a friend who can neither start nor finish a sentence...!

My world had now shrunk and I felt neither safe at home nor in school. This was about the time I stopped smiling...

Although my nanny and the servants tried as best as they could to give me the semblance of a normal life, they would still have to pick up the pieces of paper scattered all over the floor or rearrange the upturned furniture. How could one create the semblance of order and peace in a house that knew none?

My safe haven, in the midst of this miserable existence, was the chapel in the convent where I would often sit in silence during recess and thus escape the now alienation and rejection from my schoolmates. I knew deep within me that I did not need to be afraid any longer for I was in the presence of God, Jesus and the Holy Spirit and I knew that they would not hurt me!

I was after all a child, spoke like a child and prayed like a child but I somehow knew that I was being heard.

I was silent and yet, my young and childish heart was soaring across the clouds.

My mother was later diagnosed as "paranoid schizophrenic" and suffered from this illness most of her life. Medications helped but once in a while, she would regress and had to be hospitalized a few times.

My father ultimately left and remarried, thus disappearing from my life.

My tormented and painful childhood was the very thing that led me to seek God at an early age. I needed to find the peace, the love and the safety that were so lacking in my home and I will always be grateful to all the Ursuline sisters who showed me the way to the heavens and ultimately to God, Jesus and the Holy Spirit.

It was there that I found the peace, the love and the safety that I was missing. It was there that I learned, over time, to stop being a child and become His child.

I was a child, believed like a child and prayed like a child but it was then, that I began to love God, Jesus and the Holy Spirit with my whole heart. They became my true family and heaven became a home away from my house...

THREE

Alone in my room

Alone in my room
Alone here in the now
Wishing to be in a distant land
Beyond the horizon
Beyond the moon and the stars
Eyes turned toward the sun
Its warmth entering my soul
Ears bent toward the earth
Listening to the secret wisdom of old
Hands reaching up to the heavens
Hoping to see and touch eternity
Is anyone out there?
Is anyone listening?
Where is my promised land?
Where is my milk and honey?
Lips partly opened
Afraid to smile
Afraid to laugh
And yet, wanting to smile
And yet, wanting to laugh
Listening to the secret wisdom of old
Hands touching the heavens

Seeing beyond the horizon
Beyond the moon and the stars
Alone in my room
Lips partly opened
Smiling...

P.S. A lifetime ago, I was that little girl, sitting alone in her room, reaching her hands to the heavens, wanting to smile and yet, not knowing or afraid to do so!

A lifetime later, this poem was birthed within my spirit to bring her back to life, to show her the way.

Her hands are now touching the heavens. Her eyes are now seeing beyond the horizon, beyond the moon and the stars.

She is no longer afraid to smile or to laugh...

FOUR

Christmas in Versailles

I had a roof over my head and as a matter of fact, a very beautiful one! I lived in a large and sunny apartment filled with valuable antiques and paintings that were centuries old and many of our chairs and armchairs may have been beautiful, but to a child's eye, they were extremely uncomfortable! What I wanted and what I needed was a home but I really did not have one! My nanny and our servants were the only source of security and love in my life but it was not enough!

It was very hard to feel safe and secure for my mother's bouts of insanity never seemed to subside and my father was now gone most of the time. My teachers tried to be as helpful as they could but I am not sure they fully understood how unstable and traumatic my home life was. My stuttering was getting worse and my grades were now in a free fall but my parents were quite good at keeping up appearances before the world! My grandparents knew but there was very little they could do for they lived four hours away and divorce, in those days, was not an option! So I was left pretty much alone, cared for by our servants, playing with my younger brother and trying to make it from one day to the next. But I was a child, thought like a child, prayed like a child and there were very few places where I felt safe, except for the chapel. Sitting on a pew, surrounded by beautiful and colorful statues, I knew, right then and there, that I was loved. My two best friends were my dog and my cat and I liked them infinitely more than I liked people but I still remember the day my father chose to take away my dog, just because he wanted to and I cried endlessly...

If Saint Alyre was a refuge and a shelter from my volatile home environment, going to my grandparents' house for the holidays was more like going to The North Pole and visiting Mr. and Mrs. Claus!

A few days before Christmas, my father would gather everyone into the family car and off we went, at the speed of light in our fancy black Citroen, for he was a very fast driver as all Frenchmen are! Speed limits did not exist in those days and everyone drove as if they had already entered eternal life! But I knew I had not and I was always filled with dread at the sight of many approaching cars that more than often seemed to be in our lane!

We spent Christmas in Versailles, which was located near Paris, but New Year's Day was always reserved for my maternal grandparents who lived in Bois Colombes.

The Versailles days were filled with joy and laughter, good food and many gifts. They were indeed magical and while there, I would forget about my home life and be, for a few days, the happy little girl that I was created to be! As I entered my grandparent's house, I always felt as if I had just stepped into another world, a safer world! To a child's eyes, it was infinitely better and infinitely more beautiful that the North Pole could ever be! My first priority was often to go to the kitchen and ask the cook what we were having for dinner but I was almost always shoved rapidly outside the door, with a cookie in my hand. Rarely was I allowed to spend time in my grandmother's kitchen!

Although appearing stern at times, Mamie, as I called her, was very loving but made sure that her grandchildren were always polite and behaved properly. She had been raised in a very formal environment and she was simply passing on to us what she had been taught to do by her own nannies!

As I said earlier, my grandfather was a very successful banker but he had lost the use of his right arm and right hand during First World War. Because of his bravery, he had saved the lives of many of his soldiers and thus, had been made a knight by the French government! In spite of his handicap, he loved life to the fullest and being with him, was like riding a very joyous roller coaster! He looked a lot like Maurice Chevalier and was what we call in France, a "bon vivant!" To a child's eye, he was and still is as close as one gets to Saint Nicholas! I called him "bon papa" which meant "good daddy!"

Although we sang songs about "Papa Noel" and were acquainted with the North Pole, we all expected and wanted Saint Nicholas to be the one to deliver our presents and be the one to knock on our doors.

Christmas Eve was a joyous and solemn festivity in my grandparents' house and everyone, young and old, had to abide by the traditions that had been passed on for centuries. As things had been done, so were they to be done on this special evening!

Traditions, in those days, were meant to be followed and to be obeyed!

My grandmother had worked for days, carefully supervising the food preparation, the flowers and the seating arrangement. All the crystal chandeliers had been carefully dusted and each room was now bathed in golden light, as each crystal prism now became a shiny reflection of the light coming from each corner fireplace. To a child's eye, it was beautiful and magical.

One could see the joy and the pride in my grandmother's eyes for this festive occasion was her gift to us all and was meant to be enjoyed to the fullest!

My grandfather always had a small Christmas tree standing on the dining-room mantle, decorated with multi-colored lights but without a single ornament.

I often wondered at its significance but never dared to ask!

My cousins, my brother and I knew that we were expected to finish everything on our plates and suffer in silence if we happened to dislike a dish! But we all loved our roasted goose filled with chestnuts, which every French household served on Christmas Eve! We had all invented our own sign language as a way to communicate with one another without interrupting the adults' conversation. For we were not to speak unless spoken to! And so, we all waited silently for dessert, drooling over a decadent chocolate Yule log, which we called "bûche de Noël" and which we all adored.

But Christmas Eve, at my grandparents' house, was much more than eating a sumptuous meal with family and friends. It was about celebrating the birth of baby Jesus and it was about everyone attending midnight mass at the local parish. It often snowed but everyone dressed warmly and did not seem to mind walking to the church in frigid temperatures! As we all entered the large sanctuary, I was always in awe of the lights, the candles, the incense and the music, which sounded as if it had been carried down from heaven on angels' wings. I loved it and as always, I did not want it to end for as long as I was with my grandparents, I felt safe and I felt loved!

I dreaded going back to Clermont-Ferrand where,

bûche de Noël (French) : yule log (English)

once again, I would be surrounded by papers scattered across the floor and upturned furniture...!

As my father drove back to our home town, still speeding and still blind to the oncoming traffic, life seemed a tiny less gloomy for I was carrying in my arms the most beautiful porcelain doll that I had ever seen. To a child's eye, it felt as if God Himself had reached across the clouds to make a sad little girl happy for a few moments...!

FIVE

My little Franciscan grandfather

I never spent the holidays at home and I do not ever remember seeing a Christmas tree in our living room! It was in some way infinitely better for the poor tree would have had to suffer the same fate as our furniture...!

As I said in the previous chapter, we always spent Christmas in Versailles and we usually stayed there until the Feast of Epiphany. But New Year's Day was reserved for my maternal grandparents and very rarely did I have a sleepover at their house! To a child's mind, this arrangement seemed unfair and it looked as if the Bois Colombes side of the family was being punished or greatly neglected!

It took me years to realize that both sets of grandparents rarely saw each other...! But whether I spent two weeks in Versailles or a short two or three days in Bois Colombes, I loved being with them all and these days were, without any question, the happiest moments of my early life.

My maternal grandparents lived in Bois Colombes and the house where they had spent their entire lives was located in a working class neighborhood. It was a world away from the affluent and aristocratic city of Versailles, which to this day, is still as it was hundreds of years ago! But to a child's eye, it was a magical place for my grandfather had a large and beautiful rose garden which he cared for with a great deal of love and devotion and he had chickens! He taught me to care not only for his chickens but also for his rabbits and a host of other critters, which over the years, he kept on adopting! He also showed me how to tend for flowers, herbs and vegetables.

From an early age, I so wanted to be like him! I wanted to care for an entire animal kingdom and become as good a gardener as he was. My maternal grandfather was my hero and he could do no wrong!

But as they grew older, my grandparents chose to leave their beloved house, their chickens and their beautiful garden behind. I was heartbroken for I felt as if I had been kicked out of the Garden of Eden! They both moved into a small apartment. He no longer had flowers to tend to and he now had more time to devote to his religious Order and God's call on his life. For my grandfather was a Franciscan monk of the Third Order and had spent his days being devoted to a life of prayer and caring for the poor and destitute. He had created a tiny chapel in the corner of his bedroom where one could always find him, kneeling on his prayer bench before sunrise and long after sunset. As you entered his room, you felt as if you had stepped into the cell of a monastery! It probably would have looked unusual and sort of "strange" to the outside world but to a young girl who was used to it all, it was awesome! I felt as if I was back in my convent school and I loved it!

My two grandfathers could not have been more different from one another... The one from Versailles had a flamboyant and sometimes ungodly lifestyle but the one from Bois Colombes had chosen to place God first and above all, to serve others. He had made a vow of poverty, had chosen to give his money away, lead a simple existence, wear on weekends a long brown sackcloth habit and sandals on his bare feet and above all, never let go of the wooden crucifix, which he wore around his neck throughout his entire life. He was my hero!

I did have a few questions about him being a monk, being married and being a father and a grandfather but as he explained to me, Franciscan monks of the Third Order were allowed to do so.

A lifetime has gone by, but I can still see him kneeling on his prayer bench. I now know that his prayers influenced my destiny and were the force behind my life. His prayers saved me countless times and they often, but not always, prevented me from making a wrong decision or choosing a wrong path. He was and still is my spiritual giant and I am so proud to be his granddaughter!

My grandfather's ancestors came from the Basque mountains, located in the South of France. As such, he was incredibly stubborn, as most Basque people are known to be. But this quality served him well in his walk with God, in his prayer life and in his ministry to the poor. He simply refused to give up and he would keep on praying or keep on going until he received an answer from above!

Although I did not always understand why he had to wear sandals in the middle of the winter, I loved him dearly and in my eyes, he could really do no wrong for I knew he was a very special man. I knew he was a man of God!

Because of his passion for God, because of his dedication to a disciplined prayer life and because of his great devotion to the poor and destitute, you can imagine how our holidays in Bois Colombes differed from the shining festivities in Versailles! But it really did not matter for as I said, I adored my little Franciscan grandfather.

If going to Versailles felt often like sharing quarters with Mr. and Mrs. Claus, being in Bois Colombes felt as if I was in my Ursuline convent!

Although the presents were always meager, I did not mind. Being with him, whether for a day, a week or a month, was the greatest gift of all.

As we all sat down around the dinner table on New Year's Day, we knew we would be served roast beef, mashed potatoes and green beans instead of a large roasted goose stuffed with chestnuts! But we loved it all and devoured the delicious meal that my grandmother had so lovingly prepared. There were no dancing prisms floating above our heads and there was no decadent chocolate Yule log for my grandfather did not believe in having sweets for dessert... But in Versailles as well as in Bois Colombes, I knew that I was loved and that I was safe!

Once the meal was over, my grandfather always asked me to dance for him for I was still studying ballet and I loved putting on my tutu and my pink slippers. As I danced before him, in his tiny living room, I knew that these moments transcended time and would last an eternity!

In this simple and tiny living room, dressed in the brown sackcloth habit of a Franciscan monk and wearing sandals on his bare feet, he had chosen to enter, for a few moments, the world of a little girl who desperately needed to feel loved. My heart is still dancing before him...

I spent much more than a few days in his presence for there came a time when my life environment was so volatile that my grandparents judged that I would be safer being with them than being with my parents! God ordained that I would be staying in Bois Colombes instead of Versailles and I moved into a tiny spare bedroom where I was no longer surrounded by upturned furniture! I was enrolled in a new school where I felt totally alienated for I did not know a single soul but I had my grandfather! I had his love and his prayers, his help when doing my homework and for the first time in my life, I had a home where I felt safe!

But I left three months later for my parents wanted me back. Although they had gone through many counseling sessions, my mother's illness still had not subsided and my father was still gone most of the time. I knew that my future was far from being safe and still very uncertain.

And so I left Bois Colombes to go back to Clermont-Ferrand, my parents, my convent school and my big beautiful bedroom. I had left a tiny and simple apartment, which had truly been the only home I had ever known. I was now living, once again, in a palace, but to the eyes of a sad child, it was nothing more than a place to sleep and to eat. As it had been before, I had no one but God to lean on and my grandfather's prayers! To a child's eye, it was not much but it was also more than enough...!

My grandfather died peacefully in his sleep, several years later, a few feet away from his beloved prayer bench and my heart broke for I had lost my hero!

As I stared at the many priests dressed in their most festive garments and the countless Franciscan monks surrounding his casket, I truly understood how loved and revered he had been.

As I looked at the poorest of the poor, filling the pews, I realized that he had been a great help to many needy people, had managed to stay humble and fully devoted to the God he had loved and adored. To the hundreds of people sitting inside the church, he had been and was still a spiritual giant. He had been a force to be reckoned with. Although, I had big tears falling down my face, I was never as proud of my grandfather as I was on that day!

He was a spiritual giant who paved the way for his granddaughter. He gave me a heritage, which I wear with great pride.

My grandfather was a true servant who did not seek recognition from others and yet, he received it on the day of his funeral! His heart had been bigger than life itself. He had been solid as a rock and had never veered from the path God had chosen for his life for He had been stubborn and stayed stubborn until his last breath! But he had spent his entire life serving others and in doing so, He had served God!

I am still so honored to have been his granddaughter!

I am certain that when I see him again, he will be walking across the clouds, wearing a brown habit and sandals on his feet.

He will be the one to escort me all the way to the heavens and he will ask me, one more time, to dance for him!

Once again, I will dance before him...

SIX

Tuberculosis

Many things have I forgotten but many things still remain, permanently engraved in the depth of my being. Countless years have gone by and yet, these memories can still spring back to life as if it were yesterday and as if I were still there. These memories are meant to be retained and not forgotten for these were the important years. It was during these years that I became a better person, a stronger person and yet, I was just thirteen years old!

My father was still working for a large insurance company but had been recently promoted and as a result, we had left Clermont-Ferrand, the land of extinct volcanoes, quaint villages and beautiful medieval ruins which I had loved. We were now living in Caen, which, at the time, was the largest city in Normandy. This area had been utterly devastated by the Allied and German bombings and much of the city was still in ruins. Ten years had gone by since the end of the Second World War but it was hard to feel normal and lead a normal life in the midst of so much destruction. Walking to school in the midst of buildings that were no longer standing was far from being normal... As a young thirteen years old girl, I sometimes wondered if there were still bodies lying under all these ruins...! I was a war child and thought like one.

Shortly after our arrival in Caen, my mother let go of my nanny and this left me inconsolable for she had been the only stable and loving presence in my young life! I was now attending another Ursuline school but felt alienated from everyone, teachers as well as students, for I was the new kid on the block, and I still stuttered. I was also missing Saint Alyre and the nuns whom I had dearly loved and grown up with and I wished we had never left!

My world was as grey and gloomy as was the weather for it rained unceasingly. But whether the skies cooperated or not, my father loved going to Omaha Beach on weekends for being there was like going to church for him!

Not so for my mother who had supported the Vichy government, which had cooperated with the German occupying forces! She was still grieving over the fact that her hero, General Petain, had been eternally exiled to a distant and lonely island! But as I said, her insanity controlled much of her twisted thinking as well as her hateful prejudices...

I remember playing hide and seek inside many of the German bunkers that were still standing on the high dunes but were now surrounded by beautiful stands of sea oats. The massive cannons had been left behind and they were still piercing the sky through long and narrow rectangular windows as if they were ready to fight another war! The year was 1955 and my brother and I were now playing on the very dunes and beach where the Normandy invasion had taken place. But I was a young thirteen year old who was infinitely more concerned about "me" and my sad, miserable life than what had transpired on the very beach where I was now standing, playing and walking my dog! I was still unconcerned about boys for I had been, after all, raised in a convent school and watched over by loving and stern nannies!

Because of his new job, my father was gone most of the time and I was now left alone to tend for myself. My mother was still refusing to take any medications. She was beautiful, witty at times and possessed the uncanny ability to charm and fool all her psychiatrists! But she was my mother and in spite of it all, I loved her!

Within a few short weeks, we would all be leaving again for Versailles and Bois Colombes where we always spent the holidays. My two grandfathers had passed away and I knew that Christmas would not be the same without them! Losing them both had been heart wrenching and I missed especially my little Franciscan grandfather. Life was and would never be the same without him! I no longer had anyone to dance for...

Although I had suffered from a mild and chronic cough since I had moved to Normandy, no one had thought much of it and had attributed it to the cold and damp weather. But just to make sure that I was fine, my mother took me to the doctor where I had a routine TB skin test, which, a few days later, came back positive! I had somehow contracted tuberculosis and I was not only very sick, I was now highly contagious.

The enormity and the gravity of my situation never really hit me for I was only thirteen years old. I knew that people suffering from leprosy were required to be quarantined and live on far distant islands but I was not a leper! I was just a young girl who happened to cough a little more than usual!

But the health department did not budge and ordered my family to send me, within thirty days, to a mountain sanatorium.

While my grandmother scrambled to find a privately run facility, my parents tried as much as they could to make my Christmas special while I stayed "quarantined" at home! But our Christmas was far from being joyful for as each day went by, my cough kept on getting worse. My parents knew what I did not know yet! They knew that I could die! And there was no bed to be found in private sanatoriums for tuberculosis was rampant in post war France. My grandmother tried to use her influence but to no avail and I ended up being shipped to a state run facility, located in the South of France.

The fact that there were so many beds available in that particular place should have been a warning to me. I had no choice but to go there! I discovered, soon after arriving, that most of the patients came from poor working class neighborhoods. I would not only be the youngest patient, I would also be the only "rich" girl. I had entered a world, light years away from Saint Alyre, where I had been taught and required to curtsy! Blending in would not work for I stood out like a fish out of water and I knew that I was in for some rough times... But although I was now all alone, miles away from my parents and grandparents, I also knew that the prayers of my Franciscan grandfather were covering me. He may have moved up to the heavens but he was still praying for me.

The sanatorium was located in one of the most beautiful valleys of the Pyrenees, perched high up on the side of a mountain and isolated from the rest of the world for we were viewed as lepers!

Everyone was at different stages of the disease and yet curiously enough, thrown together. This did not make much sense but who was I to argue for I was quite sick and even as a young thirteen year old, I knew that I was in for the fight of my life. Seeing girls taken away from the dormitories where we all slept was not a good sign for many were never to be seen again and we all knew what that meant...! I determined early on that I would walk out and not be taken out on a stretcher! But there was a lot of mischief and fighting going on in the dormitories at night and I chose early on to close my eyes, keep my mouth shut and choose my friends and my allies carefully. Above all, I learned to keep my strength by resting as much as possible and doing whatever the doctor and the nurses told me to do. As time went on, the sanatorium became less of a prison and more of a second home away from home. It was far easier to deal with these girls than it had been to deal with my mother! I was getting stronger not only physically but also emotionally and to my great surprise, everyone now accepted me for I had learned, over time, to stand my ground and be respected!

Bed rest, pure mountain air, drinking inordinate amounts of orange juice and taking daily doses of a brand new drug called Streptomycin were the only treatments available in the fifties. We all dreaded standing each week in front of a loud and antique x-ray machine and yet, we all hoped to hear that the dark shadows in our lungs were subsiding. Death and dying were part of our existences and I lost quite a few friends during the short year that I spent there.

I was slowly getting better and my cough was almost gone but I was still required to spend six hours a day, lying in a long transatlantic chair, wrapped in warm woolen blankets, breathing the pure mountain air and listening to boring stories read by the nurses.

I was now allowed to go on daily hikes with a few nurses and the girls, who like me, were conquering tuberculosis. We sang to the top of our lungs for we all knew that we would soon be leaving, hopefully to never return again. My companions and I had gone through the fiercest battles of our lives and together, we had survived! I was discharged a few months later...

My lungs were now healthy and strong but I was no longer the young girl I used to be! The months that I had spent with my combat sisters had changed me forever! Back in Normandy, I chose to go to a different Catholic school which happened to be located in a working class neighborhood! It was there that I finally began to excel in almost all subjects and it was there that my stuttering began to subside.

My mother was as crazy as ever but I was no longer afraid of her. My father was still gone most of the time but it no longer mattered! I could have felt sorry for myself and drowned in my own tears but I chose not to. I had conquered much more than tuberculosis during the year that I had spent in the Pyrenees Mountains. It was then and there that I had learned literally to fight and become a warrior. The strength that I did not even know I had within me, would serve me well in the years to come.

As I stepped out of the sanatorium, one last time, my heart was filled with sadness for I knew that I would never see these girls again. We had fought each other countless times but we had also laughed and cried together. We had hoped and lost hope together and we had also grieved together too many times over our friends who had lost the battle!

As I looked at their faces, one last time, I knew that many would make it and that a few would not and my heart was sad, so sad...

Little did I know that what I had learned in the beautiful Pyrenees Mountains would soon be put to the test in other mountains.

But this is another chapter, another story.

SEVEN

Ski Accident

Many years had gone by since the end of the Second World War and France looked and acted, on the surface, as if there had never been one! But everyone knew and remembered that thousands of lives had disappeared from the face of the earth! Many had gone on a one-way trip to the gas chambers or concentration camps. Others had been tortured and shot dead by the Gestapo and the rest had either survived or been blown to pieces by Allied and German bombs! To the families who had lost their loved ones, life would never been the same. To the others, music was once again in the air. If France was way past Josephine Baker, it was now in love with Elvis Presley and his swaying hips

The open-air markets were once again filled with colorful fruits, vegetables, all kinds of meat, fowl and sausages and one could, from a distance away, enjoy the familiar smell of various pungent cheeses. Life was back to normal for the cooking goddesses that French women had been created to be! Going away for the weekend was slowly and surely replacing going to church on Sundays for now that things were almost back to normal, God was no longer needed! The countryside was once again the sanctuary of choice for many Frenchmen!

I was a normal seventeen year old French teenager who loved Roy Orbison, Gilbert Becaud and Paul Anka and I wore my bikinis with a great deal of pride and satisfaction!

We were now living in Grenoble and I had chosen to attend public school. I was done, once for all, with religious school and I wanted to fly my own wings and set my own course! I no longer talked about God for this was certainly not cool among my new friends. Neither did I want to be seen as the good Catholic girl who had spent her whole life kneeling and praying in convents. In order to graduate and conquer the much dreaded and highly competitive baccalaureate exam, I had chosen philosophy, literature and foreign languages as my primary subjects and I could not wait to face my examiners, be done with high school and register at the local university!

Existentialism had become my religion of choice and although it was only a fleeting fad, it affected me greatly for I stopped going to church on Sundays. But I was, above all, a seventeen year old girl who wondered how it would feel to be kissed for the very first time...! Boys were now more often on my radar than Jean Paul Sartre and Albert Camus.

Because of my new passion for existentialism, I had pledged allegiance to a new creed and a new set of doctrines, which rejected God's existence or viewed Him as the fruit of people's fertile imaginations. It looked as if I were a long way from what I had learned and experienced in my Ursuline convent but my religious beliefs were really not gone. They were simply hidden and waiting for the right time to come out! Although God's voice was now silent in my heart, He had not left and He was still calling me from the deep and watching over me, in spite of me!

But who needs God when you are young, pretty and you have a full and promising life ahead of you...?

I had stopped studying ballet for I just wanted to have fun! I was now dancing to the sound of Fats Domino who was the rage among French teenagers at the time.

I loved living in Grenoble for not only was it beautiful but it was also located in the middle of the French Alps, surrounded by mountains and glaciers.

It was there that I developed a passion for climbing and skiing and this love has never subsided for my heart still beats faster when I see mountain ranges covered in glistening snow. I felt as if they were calling me every morning as I opened my window shutters and they are still calling me a lifetime later! My heart has always been and still is in the mountains!

When I was not in school, I was either skiing or climbing. When there was no longer any snow to be found at lower altitudes, I would go higher! It was incredibly beautiful but it was also treacherous for there were many hidden dangers. Although I knew the terrain where I was skied, I was also aware that I was at the mercy of a snow-covered crevasse or a sudden powerful avalanche. I may have been a dare devil but I had no intention of dying early and I had learned where to ski and not to ski!

My grades were of course falling for I was spending much more time skiing than studying but I always seemed to make up for lost time by the end of each semester, except for physics and chemistry! This drove my teachers crazy but my parents did not seem to care for they had their own marital problems and their lives to deal with. As I had been most of my life, I was still alone. God was no longer on the main stage of my destiny for I had pushed Him into the wings! But He was waiting for the right moment, the right time to show me that He was still my God...

My friends and I went skiing every weekend, taking risks and loving it for we were all young, bold, expert skiers and yet, sometimes unwise!

It was late spring and we all knew that the risk of avalanches was particularly high on that day and because of this potential risk, we had chosen a new route!

But as if forewarned by a force from high above the clouds, I chose to leave the group and went down alone on a less thrilling and less brilliant but safer route. Within a few minutes, a huge chunk of snow and ice broke off the mountain, thus creating a massive avalanche, which swept everyone away. They all survived except for a friend of mine who died instantly!

I often wondered if she would have followed me if I had asked her to do so! Probably not, for she was a thrill addict and a much better skier than I was. She would have probably trusted her judgment and not mine.

This tragedy should have dissuaded me from ever skiing again but it did not and I was back on the slopes the following weekend! Although grieving, I did not want fear to paralyze me and I was, in some way, skiing for her.

It was the end of the afternoon and the snow was rapidly and dangerously turning into ice and I knew that I needed to get off the slopes as fast as possible.

I was approaching an area where skiers usually congregated to drink hot cocoa, cider or hot rum as most French people do in the midst of their day of skiing!

These beverages would certainly help them go down the mountain a little bit faster but would not make them necessarily safer...

A woman chose to step away from the group and started to ski in my direction, totally oblivious to the fact that she was now in my downhill path. I chose to swerve to the left so as not to hit her but in doing so, I ran into a Poma lift, which to this day, I do not remember ever seeing! But I will never forget the sound of the lift striking my head! It felt as if a thousand bells had suddenly chosen to land inside my head and ring at the same time...! I fell to the ground, unable to stand and unable to hear anything except for the loud and dreadful bells which were still ringing inside my brain.

People rushed to my aid and offered me, out of all things, a glass of rum! This was probably one of the worst things to do after a head injury but I was in France and alcohol has always been and still is the preferred remedy to many ailments!

I was far too young to know any better and incapable, at the moment, to make a rational decision but I knew, deep down, that I had been hurt badly. I managed to make it all the way back down to the parking lot at the speed of a skiing turtle, if ever there was such a creature!

The only thing I wanted to do was to crawl into my bed and try to forget that this day had ever happened. But no such luck!

The headaches kept on getting worse but curiously enough, no one saw the need to take me to the hospital and have me checked by a neurologist. Everybody assumed that bed rest would do the trick! And yet, within a few days, I lost consciousness and did not regain it until I was in the emergency room.

I had indeed suffered a massive trauma to the left side of my brain and would keep on losing consciousness in the weeks to come. Because of my injury, I lost not only the ability to read but also to speak fluently for as time went by, I discovered that a great many words seemed to have been obliterated from my memory bank.

My recovery was long and tedious but there came a day when doctors finally allowed me to read again. With the help of many children's books, my vocabulary slowly enlarged, but I was a long way from Jean Paul Sartre and Albert Camus!

Tintin and Bécassine are still, to this day, my favorite children's books!

I kept on improving and as time went by, there were fewer and fewer words that seemed to be missing from my French vocabulary. Little did I know, at the time, that I would, one day, in the not so distant future, be using a different language where not a single word would be missing!

Exactly one year after my ski accident, my father took time away from his busy schedule to take me back to the place where it had all happened and he encouraged me to ski downhill once again! He did not want fear to get a hold on me and he knew that if I did not conquer my demons, I would never ski again. He stayed near and watched as I started to go downhill ever so slowly, at the speed of a skiing turtle! On that day and at that moment, he was more of a dad to me that he had ever been and would ever be...

With the help of my teachers and my friends, I received my Baccalaureate Degree the following year and graduated with a major in philosophy.

I was alive but I still had a long way to go for I still had countless words missing inside my brain...!

I was alive but I was no longer the girl I used to be...

EIGHT

L' Alpe d' Huez

If my stubbornness and strong determination had been of great help before, there was little they could do now to stop me from having seizures and suffering from memory losses and excruciating headaches. I was seventeen years old and I felt as if my life had ended...

I do not think my mother had even begun to understand how hard I had worked at getting better. She was still as extraordinarily self-absorbed as she had ever been! My father had chosen to stay in the background and yet, I knew that they both loved me but simply did not know how to be parents and my brother, being younger than me, had a life of his own. With the help and the constant support of my friends and my teachers, I had barely passed the much-dreaded second half of my baccalaureate exam. Little did I know how well my English minor would serve me in my near future! The somewhat innocent side of my personality believed that I would be able to go to medical school but no such luck! For as I sat in the office of one of the best neurosurgeons in the country, I somehow knew that my future had been sealed by a Poma lift!

The room where I was now sitting reminded me of my grandmother's house for it was beautifully and perfectly adorned but the neurosurgeon who was about to step in was neither Saint Nick nor the bearer of good news and good gifts. I had stopped hoping that my life would return to normal and I had stopped believing in good things coming down from the heavens... I had stopped believing in a God who had promised that He would love me and watch over me...

And yet He had, for I had somehow survived a German bomb, tuberculosis, an avalanche and a brain injury! I may have felt like damaged goods but at least, I was alive! It would take me many more years to become grateful and realize how lucky and blessed I had been in the midst of my adversities. God had indeed been there and He had watched over me!

But for the moment, as I waited for the neurosurgeon to pronounce my sentence, I somehow knew that I would never be able to attend one of the local universities for I had simply lost too many words and I was no longer the girl I used to be.

"Can you draw? Can you paint?"

Could I? I had grown up surrounded by artists for my mother was an excellent watercolorist, my father was an interesting cartoonist and my grandmother excelled at playing the harpsichord. I had always loved drawing and painting but I had never planned to study at the Beaux Arts nor had I wanted to become a professional artist. This is probably why I still approach painting with a certain degree of uneasiness for in some mysterious way, it reminds me of these difficult and painful years. I should have been glad that God had already provided a solution but it was not what I had wanted to do. I had been planning to study medicine and in one sentence, the neurosurgeon had put an end to my life dream.

My life was indeed going to be different from what I had expected it to be and yet, it would surpass all my dreams and aspirations but at that moment, in time and in space, I could not help but be disappointed, hurt and angry. Where was God in all of this? He was there but I was too self-absorbed to see Him working in my life...

I wish I had stopped long enough to stop crying and instead, realize that I had been given a second chance and a way out.

Following the strong recommendations of my neurosurgeon, I enrolled at the Beaux Arts and with a divided heart, I began to study drawing and painting as I had been told to do...!

My brain injury had caused my beloved existentialist idols to fall off their pedestals. They had been forgotten and obliterated and a single blow to my head, caused by a Poma ski lift, had relegated them to the ranks of mere humans!

Since I still suffered from incapacitating headaches and seizures, my doctor advised me to let go of my studies, rest and continue to take strong barbiturates for I would not have been able to function without the help of these little pills…!

Knowing how much I loved the mountains, my father chose to rent a chalet in one of the nearby fashionable ski resorts where he thought I would be happier and hopefully, recover faster.

Showering me with gifts was my father's way of telling me that he loved me but not once, did he ever tell me that he did. These were the words that I was still hoping to hear one day but I never did! My father vanished from my life without ever telling me that I was his cherished little girl and his beloved daughter.

Although for the moment, I was no longer hearing God's voice, I had somehow always known that I was loved, cherished and watched over. This assurance would serve me well in the months to come for I was just about to step into very dangerous territories!

However beautiful and resplendent the surrounding snow-capped mountains were, I felt as if I had descended into utter darkness, for soon after moving, I discovered that many people's codes of conduct were void of morals and common decency! I am sure that there were some very nice people who lived in this beautiful ski resort but my parents' friends were untamed and their lifestyle was not only amoral but also immoral. While living there, I saw and experienced things that no seventeen year old should have been allowed to get near!

L'Alpe d'Huez was not where I would have chosen to stay for it was basically a watering hole for the very rich and the very famous who felt and looked like gods and yet, acted like devils.

I had no intention of joining their club but was forced to do so for I often found myself utterly alone and at the mercy of a few very bad "wolves" while my crazed mother was busy being wild! My father could not care less for by now, he had a life of his own and came to visit us only on rare occasions and yet, paid the bills!

As time went by, my heart and my emotions became numb and I reached a place where I no longer cared about anything or anyone. I felt used and abused and I no longer cared whether I got well or died! I had lost the will to go on and live...

Out of desperation and because of a young and cute ski instructor who had befriended me, I started to ski my heart out. As the days went by and as I got stronger, we kept on skiing higher and higher until I was strong enough to reach the land of glaciers and never ending snow where I began to feel alive again, cleansed and renewed!

I was now more than ever determined to climb out

of the rat hole I had fallen into and to reconnect to the person I used to be, if at all possible!

As I look back at this dark period of my life, I realize now how close I had come to being utterly destroyed but God's hand had been there to part the clouds that kept on surrounding me and thus, blinding me to his presence and His light!

I may have fallen a few times but I chose, one fateful day, to walk away from it all and leave behind my beautiful and yet dark surroundings.

I chose to return if at all possible, to my old life and my old friends to the utter despair of my mother who had used me to feed her demons.

I chose to return to Grenoble and trust God, one more time that He would take care of me.

I chose to return to the church of my youth and find there the safety that I used to know.

Satan may have used L'Alpe d'Huez to try to destroy me but God had instead used a young ski instructor to help me get strong and healthy enough to want out...

The prayers of my little Franciscan grandfather may not have always stopped me from choosing the dark side but they saved me from utter destruction time after time. I experienced hell and yet by God's grace, I escaped...

I chose to take a few steps back toward God and I

began to once again see His light coming from across the clouds.

The stage was now set for the miracle that was about to take place within a year.

All because of a chance encounter with two British girls while vacationing on the coast of Brittany and all because of a sailboat...

NINE

Lay your head down

Speechless
Void of emotions
Void of hopes and dreams
Not a word left
Silent
Unable to speak
Unable to hear
Heart broken like shattered glass
Millions of prisms floating in the air
Why is this happening to me?
Infinite hesitation to hope and dream
Fear of the unknown
Fear of upcoming storms
Will I be able to ride the storms?
Will I be able to stand strong?
Will I be shattered again?
Too many mountains to climb
Too many obstacles to overcome
Too many deserts to wander in
Where is the promised land of milk and honey?
Why can't I cross the waters?

And if I do
What will I find there?
Unfamiliar landscape filled with giants
Will I hear a small voice coming from afar?
Will I hear it whisper?
You are home now
It took you a while
You took countless detours
Rest and look around
The giants are now gone
Spring has finally come
Listen!
The brook is bubbling
The roses are blooming
Lay your head down
Rest

TEN
Summer in Brittany

Several years had gone by since my brain injury and most of them had been spent partying and basically wasting my life away! I had witnessed things that no one should be allowed to see or be involved in! I may have been a young and innocent seventeen-year-old when I had been encouraged by my mother to "spread my wings," but my lifestyle had slowly caused me to die emotionally and spiritually. I had sometimes considered suicide as a way out of the hell I was now living in...! These beautiful people had been nothing more than demons disguised as gods and goddesses!

Even now, as a lifetime has gone by, I still have great difficulties revisiting these dark places of my life...!

Three years had gone by but my heart was now numb and I often felt as if I were a mere shell...

But I still loved skiing and being on the high mountain slopes. This enabled me to escape the sordid reality of my existence, to feel clean once again and dare to believe that I could get away from the Sodom and Gomorrah where I had spent two miserable years.

I know that the prayers of my Franciscan grandfather gave me, one day, the courage to walk away and never return!

My heart may have been numb, but my strong willpower was still set on being the ultimate "leader of my pack," and helping me return to a normal lifestyle!

My emotions may have been shattered, but I was determined to rediscover the decent person I used to be and to lead a "normal" life if at all possible!

I was more alone than I had ever been for my parents were slowly and steadily heading for a divorce. Although they were still living under the same roof, they were no longer husband and wife and had relationships of their own!

Back in Grenoble, I began to take a few art classes and to mingle, once again, with my old friends who by now had gone on to various graduate schools. I often felt inadequate in their presence for the only thing I had to show for myself was two years of happy partying and an often sad and desperate lifestyle...! Many were close to embarking on exciting careers and my only achievements were a few good drawings and several "not so good" paintings! My mother was still angry with me for having chosen to depart from Sodom and Gomorrah and her many party friends! My father had happily pulled the financial plug and in doing so, had basically shipped her back home where she belonged but did not want to be!

But rain or shine, as my family had always done throughout the course of our lives, we left in June to spend the summer in Brittany, on the Cote-d'Armor!

Grenoble was a long way from the western coast of France and as much as I was looking forward to going back to a land which I had loved throughout my childhood, I still dreaded sitting in the back of the car and watching my father pass every car that dared to be in his way! If there were speed limits, he certainly chose not to respect them and drove as if he were racing against time itself...

Brittany was and still is a beautiful and mysterious corner of the French landscape!

It is a magical land of menhirs, dolmens, druid legends and magical tales. It is an enchanting land where the sea resembles the color of a perfect emerald and where each afternoon, the granite shoreline turns pink and vermillion as the setting sun adorns its rocky coastline.

It was there that I saw, countless times, the mysterious "green flash" while watching the western sun go down beyond the horizon.

My father loved spending his summers in Brittany and one could always find him, sitting in a quiet area of the beach, smoking his pipe and reading a good book. To him, it was as close to heaven as he could get!

My mother, on the contrary, found these summers dull and utterly boring. Because of her displeasure, her rage episodes always seemed to increase in frequency and intensity. This led me to be embarrassed and afraid to encounter one of our summer neighbors on the street!

If I had made steady physical improvements over the past three years, I would still, once in a while, stumble upon a word or two that seemed to have been permanently erased from my memory bank, but I had slowly learned to work around this hurdle. My small seizures and still excruciating headaches were comfortably controlled by daily heavy doses of Phenobarbital!

I may have looked good on the outside but on the inside, I was nothing more than a wreck, dreading to meet all the friends I had spent previous summers with. I was trying to relearn how to behave among normal and decent people and more than often, I felt very much older than my young age…

If skiing had been my salvation from Sodom and Gomorrah, sailing was going to be my way to become the person I desperately wanted to be! Going back to church did not help me for as I said before, my heart was numb and I doubted that God could or would ever love me again… Going to confession did not help either for I found it to be an empty ritual which, in no way, helped bring forth the healing that I needed to receive from high above.

Little did I know that God had never left me, but I had chosen to leave Him!

Little did I know that He had watched over me and prevented my utter destruction!

But it was very hard to find my footing again and I was finding myself running back to Him at the speed of a very slow turtle instead of a racing rabbit.

I knew that the world of the "so-called" beautiful people was now dead to me and I saw this summer as a welcome respite between who I used to be and who I hoped to become.

This summer afforded me the time to sail and I spent most of my days on the water, in good and in bad weather. I still did not have a boat, but my friends often asked me to come along for they knew that I was a very good sailor and always willing to be their crewmate. As much as I loved riding the waves with them, deep down I wanted to be the captain of my own ship!

A few weeks after our arrival in Brittany, my father left early one day and came back, many hours later, with a shiny sailboat, sitting on top of a brand new trailer. I wish you could have seen my mother's reaction! She probably thought of all the clothes she could have bought and all the trips she could have taken with the money that my father had just chosen to spend...! But this was to be his new toy for the time being and I kept on sailing with my friends...

I soon discovered that my father spent quite a bit of time more in the water than inside his boat for he kept on capsizing! Unwilling to take lessons since he was on vacation, the amusement soon wore off. He chose to return to the beach where, once again, one could find him, smoking his pipe and reading a good book. I wish I had been given a chance to know him better and to let him know that I loved him, but I was never allowed to step through that door which stayed shut for the remainder of his earthly life.

I, of course, inherited the brand new sailboat and my friends were now the ones coming along...

My sailing companions knew of my brain injury, but no one knew the way I had spent the last two years of my life. It was a dark season, which I chose to keep hidden from everyone. It was a dark world, which I chose not to reveal or talk about to anyone.

As far as they were concerned, I was the same person as I had always been.

As far as I was concerned, I was no longer the person I used to be!

This suited me well enough for I was intent on forgetting my past, if at all possible...

So I sailed, danced, ate freshly picked oysters and clams, drank white wine, played bridge and tried to solve world problems through long and heated nightly discussions. After all, we were French and this was what young and decent French college and graduate students did when on vacation! Many had already entered medical or law schools and prestigious "Grandes Ecoles"!

All the guys had brains but they also had raging hormones. When not on the water, one of their favorite occupations was to ogle girls walking by and try to recruit the prettiest ones into our clan.

The game was always on and our numbers were soon enlarged by the arrival of two bikini-clad goddesses from the British Isles! Although we all spoke English, we were certainly far from being fluent and it was quite amusing to observe the language skills of these smart and handsome young men improve at the speed of light.

I did not know, at the time, that these two girls would be instrumental in altering the course of my life, my destiny and somehow, help me know eternity!

As the summer went by, I kept on getting stronger, feeling washed and cleansed by the long hours that I had spent on the water and by the time that I had spent in my old friends' carefree and wholesome company.

But good things often have to come to an end and I soon found myself on the way back to Grenoble, back to an unknown and somewhat uncertain future. It was the last time I saw my childhood friends for soon after, life would take me halfway across a vast ocean and far from this land of enchantment that I had always loved.

I returned to Brittany and the Cote-d'Armor a lifetime later. My hair was gray and I was now a grandmother with six grandchildren. I had neither died emotionally nor physically and my heart was now no longer numb for, over the course of a long life, I had found my way back to God and back to His love.

But for the moment, as it had been each summer of long ago, I fell in love, once again, with this magical and mysterious land where, as a child and then, as a broken young woman, I used to sit on a pink granite boulder, waiting for the green flash to appear above the horizon. I was now in my sixties but in my heart, I was still the young girl who sailed across these waters in good and in bad weather...

I could almost see her, sailing in the far distance, happy and carefree, surrounded by green and turquoise transparent waters, carrying a happy smile on her face, loving life and loving God...

ELEVEN

Fall of 1964

Fall was in the air and it was just a matter of weeks before my beloved mountains would turn white, thus announcing the arrival of another exciting ski season.

Being on the slopes had always been my escape from my intensely troubled family environment, which is why I had chosen to continue skiing in spite of my brain injury and my near encounter with a deadly avalanche!

I was back at the Beaux Arts, but not enjoying it for I felt as if this career path had been pushed down my throat! I was painting and drawing and yet, my life was far from being satisfying and as a result, many of my art projects were left unfinished.

There had to be more to life than spending hours in front of a large easel! How could I truly fill canvases with glorious and vibrant colors when my heart was still as numb and dead as ever! I was nothing more than a shell and if I had ever owned creative juices, they now had dried up! I also felt often as if I were a referee, arbitrating a fight unto death between the left and the right side of my brain... As I said, my heart was not into being or even becoming an artist and yet, I was! It took a great many years to realize and accept the fact that I had been born an artist and have always looked at life as an artist. I just did not know it back then for I was concentrating on getting well and trying to forget the last few miserable years of my life! I still had many questions for the heavens above but, so far, had received no answers. Spending the summer in Brittany had been a wonderful breath of fresh air which I had not experienced in quite a while. I was now back in Grenoble, living with my mother and feeling totally alone, alienated from my old friends who had gone on to graduate schools and had a life of their own.

I had decided to go back to church, attend masses regularly and become once again, a good and proper Catholic girl as if such a thing were possible now! Being obedient to a system that had been in place for hundreds of years brought me a much-needed solace and a small degree of peace in the midst of a volatile and sometimes violent home situation. My mother's mental illness had not subsided and she was still as unstable as she had ever been. My exquisite, witty and charming mother had mastered the art of wrapping all her psychiatrists around her beautifully manicured small fingers and as long as she was happy, they were happy! She probably would have been able to charm a cobra.

Being in church, as it had been in my convent days,

and would be throughout my life, offered me a place of refuge from the many storms I was still facing. I felt safe but the passion that I used to have and share with my Franciscan grandfather was now long gone. My heart was thirsting for something that I could not even put a name to. The many "bad boys" I had met over the last two years of my life had left me feeling empty. No one was there to show me the way for French people are and have always been very private about the affairs of their hearts. And as a matter of fact, they do not talk much about other "affairs" either...!

Going to church was good enough for the time being but it was simply not enough. God seemed now distant and aloof and I honestly missed Him, but did not know how to bring Him down to my level, my heart and my life!

Three years had now gone by since my brain injury and I had become addicted to barbiturates for I was still suffering from excruciating headaches. My speech was "normal" except for the thousands of words that had been permanently obliterated from my memory's vault but who needed them anyway...!

I was meeting regularly with the priest of my local church to talk about my past, my present and my future but I honestly thought that there was very little he could do to help a young woman whose life had been destroyed by a Poma lift, while skiing high up in the French Alps. And yet, as young and somewhat inexperienced as he appeared to be, he kept on reminding me that God had refused to see me die and had stubbornly chosen to preserve my life countless times! He had rescued me from a German bomb, healed me from tuberculosis, prevented me from being swept away by a falling avalanche and had given me the strength and the courage to walk away from an enticing and glittering hell! This young and not so inexperienced priest began to show me how self-pity had now entrapped me and how angry I was at God and my parents. He helped me sort out my feelings and held my hands as I began to walk slowly and hesitantly on a redemptive path.

Everything in me wanted to bring back the person I used to be before my brain injury but I could not for I had let my heart and my emotions vanish for a little while in the land of the beautiful people. I now was more determined than ever to regain access to the God who had so tenderly loved me through my childhood and my early life. He had been the force behind the tears I had cried as a child and He, alone, had given me the courage to walk away from l'Alpe d'Huez!

Skiing and sailing may have helped but ultimately, my heart had chosen to make a 360° turn and reconnect to Him, His presence and His voice!

I was no longer the person I used to be and I was slowly learning to accept, get acquainted with and love the new me! I was beginning to understand and realize that my life was far from being over for although I still had hundreds of words still missing in the deep recesses of my brain, there were a great many more that I had not forgotten!

This was a slow and tedious task but this kind and gentle priest had helped me a great deal and in some mysterious and timely way, had prepared me for my future...

One fateful evening, in the fall of 1964, two American girls whom I had never met, showed up on my doorstep! While in Paris, they had met my two bikini-clad goddesses from the British Isles who had given them my name and address! These two strangers went on to explain that they were about to embark on a yearlong course of study at the University of Grenoble...!

French people are often reluctant to open their doors to foreigners for they see their homes as forbidden or restricted fortresses! As a result, many of the foreign students ended up never meeting or knowing the "natives"! They often spent more time speaking English than French...! Many would go home without having ever experienced what life in a French home was all about. Mine was not exactly a healthy example, but my parents were truly gifted at putting up a front when they wanted to!

Grenoble was a very large and vibrant cosmopolitan city, a world away from Montana and upstate New York where these two young American women were from.

I was having a somewhat difficult time adjusting to their casual and laissez-faire approach to life in general for I found their social customs to be a little bit too relaxed and perplexing and their ways to pronounce the English language peculiar...

But their arrival had provided a much-needed exotic distraction to my life, which, I still viewed as boring unless I went skiing. All the Alpine resorts were now opened and it promised to be a long season for there was already plenty of snow and winter had not even arrived yet.

As time went by, my two new friends kept on getting more and more homesick for the holidays were soon approaching and through them, I became acquainted with a new chapter of American History 101!

I knew infinitely more about the American Revolution, General Lafayette and the Civil war than Thanksgiving! I was just about to get acquainted with a holiday that seemed to be supremely and almost religiously important to my two new friends but had absolutely no significance for the French population at large...

I knew very little about Native Americans other than what I had learned from John Wayne! And the brave souls, who had crossed the Atlantic Ocean at the worst possible time of the year and landed in Plymouth, were still strangers to me!

But since this holiday seemed to be of great

significance to these American girls, I decided to have a party in their honor and offer them the French version of a typical Thanksgiving dinner if such a thing could ever be possible to cook and recreate!

Little did I know that this fateful Thanksgiving dinner would change my fate and my destiny?

Little did I know that one year from now, I would also cross the Atlantic Ocean, at the worst possible time of the year, and land not too far from Plymouth...?

TWELVE

A new destiny

I soon discovered that preparing a Thanksgiving feast in Grenoble, France, was easier said than done for no one had ever heard of cranberry sauce, pumpkin pies and yams smothered in pecans, brown sugar and marshmallows!

I was living in a centuries old land of baguettes where one does not just go buy bread! One enters religiously the local bakery as if it were a sanctuary and proceeds to examine carefully each and every baguette so as to choose the perfect one and take it home with pride, satisfaction and a great deal of anticipation! This lifestyle has a way to slow you down and helps you enjoy the simplest details when it comes to France and French cooking.

It is the land, after all, where Julia Child started a lifelong affair with beef bourguignon and chocolate mousse and where every woman was born to be a true cooking goddess.

French people see cooking as much more than a task to perform. They see it as an art!

But on the night of this festive American occasion, we did have the required roasted turkey and a vast array of delicious French dishes! It was indeed a multicultural evening and my two new friends seemed to enjoy themselves immensely. Montana and Upper New York State evaporated quickly when they found themselves sitting next to adoring male friends of mine who found nothing more exciting than to practice their English skills, while eating dinner!

As for me, I could not take my eyes off the tall and handsome young American who was sitting across the dining room table. He had the most beautiful green eyes that I had ever seen, but he seemed shy and detached from the rest of the group. His name was Don, which for the life of me, I could not pronounce correctly.

I learned later that he was a top skier, a guide at Mount Rainier and had chosen the University of Grenoble because of its location in the midst of the French Alps!

I was hooked!

My Thanksgiving friends and I decided to go and spend two weeks near Chamonix where skiing would be treacherous but thrilling. I had asked, of course, Don to come along for I really wanted to know him better and I was also dying to find out if he liked me as much as I liked him.

As the old raggedy bus took us all to our destination,

I was sitting next to a tall and handsome mountain climber from Seattle. This was really the first time we had talked to each other and we both knew right away that we shared a deep passion for the mountains, skiing and climbing.

I was even more hooked now...!

As we all gathered that evening and sat around a long and rustic dining room table, I was still next to him! Little did he know how determined I was for I would have killed if anybody had dared to sit next to him!

As we all went dancing, a few nights later, Don finally invited me to dance, took me in his arms, kissed me and the rest is history!

I was hooked for life...!

My life as a single young woman had just ended and I did not want Don to ever let go of me!

In a crazy and surreal way, I knew that I would be by his side for the rest of eternity and yet, we barely knew each other. We were both swept by a torrent of emotions that neither one of us had ever known or experienced, and we felt as if we had both stepped into a magical land where the cares of this world no longer existed! Don was still, in many ways, a stranger to me such as I probably was to him but I felt safe when I was with him.

Although he was five years younger than me, he was

in many ways older than his age, for he had spent a great deal of time climbing with highly respected mountain climbers and these older men had helped form his strong character.

We spent the next two weeks talking, holding hands, walking on beautiful snow-covered roads and kissing every chance we got.

There was no need to hide my past if our relationship was meant to flourish and I wanted him to know the real me, without the help of false pretenses and lies! It was not easy, but I had no choice and we kept on talking about our individual lives, our dreams and our goals. If my life had looked golden from the outside, it had also been incredibly more painful than his and I wanted him to know, from the beginning of our relationship, what he was really getting into. Honesty was the key to our survival for I was still hooked on barbiturates and uncertain about who I would become and what I would end up accomplishing, in spite of or because of my brain injury! Don had a bright future ahead of him for he would be attending Yale University a few months from now. My life was still a big blur...I was an artist with plenty of unfinished canvases...!

But at that moment and in the midst of our idyllic surroundings, it did not matter for we were young, innocent, falling in love at the speed of light and we both knew that there was no turning back! I had difficulties envisioning my life without him and neither could he!

We skied and climbed a few mountains for the next six months and I discovered that he was indeed a top skier and a remarkable and trustworthy mountain guide. I felt safe while attached to his rope and I would have probably tried to climb the North face of the Eiger if he had wanted me to...! We did not always reach the summit of the many mountains we tried to climb for we spent way too much time kissing along the way...!

He may have been younger than me but he was able to do what no other doctor had been able to do until then. He helped me kick not only my Phenobarbital habit but also stop smoking!

Don flew back to Seattle, Washington in June 1965 and spent the following summer guiding people to the top of Mount Rainier and saving a few lives along the way. For the first time in my life, I worked as a camp counselor, which I truly enjoyed.

I was destined to leave soon after for England where my father had planned to send me but I chose instead to embark on a much longer voyage. I chose to cross the Atlantic Ocean in the fall of 1965, stop being a wanderer and embark on a pilgrimage, seeking a life with Don and seeking God.

As I look back at this extraordinary chain of events, I cannot help but see the hand of a merciful God at work not only in my life but also in Don's!

God knew that we were both very young, somewhat innocent, very much in love and determined to stay together and make it to the end.

We had become much more than a skiing and a climbing team in the French Alps. We had become a life team and God must have known that nothing would ever be able to break the rope that, unbeknown to us at the time, He Himself had tied around our lives and our hearts.

Being safely loved by Don had enabled me to soften my heart and open it once again to God and the realization that He had always been there watching over me and being the father and the mother that I had never had. He may not have always liked what I had chosen to do but I somehow knew that He had always loved me!

Because of Don, I dared to believe in a better future and because of God, I dared to welcome His future for me and for us!

November 23rd, 1964 had been much more than a festive Thanksgiving meal shared with good friends. It had been a divine appointment with the author and the finisher of my life!

As I look back at this fateful evening, I already knew that, somehow, I would be by this tall and handsome stranger's side not only for the rest of my life but also for the rest of eternity and yet, we had only met!

THIRTEEN

" Ellis Island "

God alone knows the extent of the price I paid by following Don to the United States and embarking on a lone journey across a vast ocean.

I left behind a family which, as imperfect as it had been, was the only one I had ever known.

I left behind a brother who, from now on, I would only see on extremely rare occasions and two beloved grandmothers who knew that they would never see me again.

I left my little dog, Chou, who had been my faithful companion when hiking and climbing. To this day, I cannot see a small four-legged black critter without crying silent tears...

I left the church of my youth for little did I know, that I would never experience again the sacramental beauty of a Latin Mass.

I left my childhood toys, my beautiful porcelain doll and the many books I had loved devouring for they had often been my only way to escape life and a painful home environment.

I left a land that I had loved passionately for while I grew up there, the French Alps and Brittany had offered me a home away from home. There I had felt God's presence and love. There I had grown stronger and recovered from my brain injury!

I left France with a host of happy and sad memories, two small suitcases and a canvas backpack in my hand, not knowing what my future would hold and where it would ultimately take me...

As I stood on the stern of the ship, which was taking me away from France, I felt very much like Ruth, a beloved character from the Old Testament.

Don's land would be my land! His people would be my people but contrary to the story, I was determined that my God would become His God...!

But as Boaz had ultimately redeemed Ruth's life, Don had already begun to do so in the early stage of our relationship and would continue to do so in the years to come...

But at this very moment, there was so much unknown about the land I was about to enter and the people I was about to connect with, that it prevented me from being afraid. I simply did not know what I was supposed to fear! I was blissfully ignorant about the potential dangers that I could and would face as a young woman, who, four days from now, would set foot on another continent.

But at this very moment, I was crying and saying goodbye to the land and the people I had loved. I was saying goodbye to my life as I had known it to be.

After a while, I chose to stop staring at the horizon, turned my face away from the disappearing French coastline, and stepped back inside the ship.

I chose to wait, four long days, for a new world and a new life to rise above a different horizon...

The crossing was uneventful but it often felt surreal for you need to realize that I had never left home and I was now surrounded by countless Americans and people of various nationalities!

I may have been on the stern of the ship four days ago but I now was standing on its bow, staring with wonder and amazement at the coastline of the United States slowly approaching in the distance. Mile by mile, I was getting nearer a world which I really knew very little about, other than the information I had gathered in school.

I was entering this foreign land on a visitor visa which would enable me to travel, take a few classes and would require me to return to France nine months from now. But I had really no intention to do so and I already knew that I would have to learn to skillfully navigate the immigration system in order to find the magical road to a green card!

I still possessed the feisty iron will of many of my ancestors who, centuries ago, had been lords, knights and had fought countless battles without ever wanting to lose a single one! Neither was it my intention to lose…! Having a visitor visa was priceless but it prevented me to ever work and earn a living. However, my father had offered to help me financially for the extent of my "visit!"

But the ship had finally docked and as we stood in line, waiting to be interviewed by immigration officers, I could not help but keep my eyes on Don who was standing against the walls of a nondescript concrete and steel building. I wanted to run into his arms, feel safe and step into his world!

No such luck for the entire immigration proceedings took hours and it was then and there that I began to develop an intense dislike for these stern and somewhat threatening federal employees!

Within a few hours of my arrival to New York City, which I had found to be dirty, I travelled to New England where I was supposed to spend the next nine months as an au pair! I had signed my name on the dotted line without truly knowing what an "au pair" meant and I wished I had done so, for my living arrangements turned out to be an absolute disaster… From a girl who had spent her early years surrounded by servants and nannies, I was now treated, as if my first name was Cinderella and not Daniele!

Between, cleaning, doing laundry, making beds and cleaning dishes, I somehow managed to take a few

English classes at the local university, which would serve me well in the years to come.

My school schedule, my upbringing and my financially independent status caused a lot of friction, which, unfortunately, was impossible to remedy! This situation left me no recourse but to pack my two suitcases, my canvas backpack, leave without a second thought and yet, jump into a very uncertain future.

I may have felt like the little Heidi when I had lived in the French Alps, but I had no intention of being a Franco-American Cinderella...

My situation was precarious for the people I had stayed with for a few short and somewhat difficult months were no longer my sponsors. They, soon after, called the Immigration Services to inform them of my departure which left me exactly thirty days to find another au pair situation since my visa did not allow me to find a regular job.

I have always found this situation somewhat peculiar since my father was the only person who was covering the entire cost of my stay in the United States. My father was, in fact, my real and only sponsor, but who was I to argue with a foreign federal agency, which, over the next few years, I would learn not only to dread but also enjoy circumventing on countless occasions...!

As I said, my situation was precarious but not hopeless for God was on my side...!

I was becoming more and more aware that I would have to be the one fighting for the survival of my relationship to Don.

My "Prince Charming" was enrolled at Yale University and had started his freshman year, which made it impossible and unwise for him to take time away from his studies and help me. And yet, he did as much as he could! I knew in my heart that he was worth all the efforts I would have to make and all the battles I would have to wage to be able to stay in this somewhat unfriendly land where I had not felt very welcomed.

Much remained to be known and much remained to be unveiled but it did not matter for I was willing to wait four years...

God had tied an unbreakable rope around our hearts, in the midst of my beautiful French Alps and I was willing to fight for the survival of our passionate love affair.

Because of God's love and ultimate purpose for both of our lives, and in spite of our innocence, we were a formidable force that transcended time and space.

But for the time being, I would be the one who would have to fight, in the midst of a foreign land, a foreign culture and the Immigration "KGB"!

FOURTEEN

Yale Campus

Although Don and I had seen each other almost every weekend during my short au pair career, I knew that he could not help me for he was a full-time student at Yale University. He really did not possess the know how to navigate the immigration system and help me solve my present visa hurdles! Neither did I... But God must have known for He intervened at what looked like the last hour...

Little did I know that by answering a solitary ad in the New York Times, I would be delivered from all my immigration difficulties and find another sponsor! I had discovered that the name "Yale University" carried much weight and although this family had never met me, they had been nice enough to trust a perfect stranger into their home, which happened to be located in Manhattan. A few phone calls from Don's friends had eloquently helped convincing them to give me a chance!

They were quite wealthy and lived in a grandiose East Side penthouse, straight across from the United Nations. I had never ridden a private elevator nor had I tended beautiful flowers, located on terraces, while standing on the top floor of a high rise! I was required to help with the household but I did not mind for they were kind, considerate, and very intelligent. They treated me as if I was a member of the family and this was a world away from what I had experienced in New England!

I was to oversee the care of their two adorable little girls, walk them to school every day and basically be their nanny in Manhattan as well as in West Hampton where they had a summer house. The roles had indeed been reversed, but I did not mind for it allowed me to see Don and stay in the United States.

I was still spending weekends at Yale University but I was having a difficult time adjusting to an Ivy League campus lifestyle!

Don and I were very much in love and a world away from weekly frenetic mixers that seemed to center on heavy drinking and wild partying. We still loved outdoor activities and spent many weekends rock climbing in Western Connecticut.

As I look back at my life through the writing of this book, I find amusing that I was now the girl who could no longer stand partying! Although I had often been a more than willing participant, I was no longer interested!

To my French eyes, life on the all male Yale campus was irritating and very superficial. Students basically went to classes on weekdays but got drunk on weekends while hosting girls from nearby Ivy League colleges! It often felt as if I had been transported into the world of the "Great Gatsby" but I was not Daisy Buchanan and my wild days were long gone! As he had done for several years, Don left the East Coast, early in June, to go back to Mount Rainier, work as a guide during the summer months and save a few more lives.

I followed my host family to the Hamptons and I truly was, for the first time in a very long time, enjoying my life. I divided my time between caring for the children, whom I now dearly loved, and reading good books on my days off.

Little did I know that the peace I was now experiencing would soon be shattered and thrown to the wind? Once again, my life was about to explode!

My two adorable little companions had gone on to play at a friend's house and as they were waiting to cross the street, the youngest one decided to dash forward unto the path of an oncoming vehicle. There was never any traffic on this road but on that day, the sun had been so bright that the oncoming driver never saw her and neither did she see him…! She did not suffer for she died instantly.

Since it had been my day off, I had chosen to spend the day on the beach and to read a good book.

Both parents descended into annihilation for so deep was their grief and so visceral was their pain. As many of their relatives kept on moving in, I realized that I did not belong there. Although they had treated me as one of their own, I really was not! They did not need my help any longer and I knew that it was just a matter of days before I would have to leave. Shortly after, everyone agreed that it was time to pack my bags and move on.

So I left and found myself alone and grieving for the death of this beautiful little girl.

I was angry with God for having allowed this tragedy to happen...

I also knew that, once again, I would have to deal with the Immigration Services for I only had thirty days to find another family and another sponsor.

But I was also burned out, tired and I no longer had the energy nor the willpower to hunt for another solution to my immigration hurdles. I felt as if I had reached the end of my rope!

Flying back to France sounded almost like a relief!

I went up, one last time, to the penthouse where I had truly been happy, and while putting away my belongings, I looked at the United Nations across the street.

Although I spoke three different languages, I had never, absolutely never, envisioned myself crossing the street, stepping inside this imposing tower and asking if they had a job for me...

Even now, as I type these words, I cannot help but smile and wonder...

Did I really, really do that?

I did but as always, an invisible and yet invincible force had been behind me...!

God Himself must have placed an invisible, tiny and yet supernaturally invincible seed of faith in my heart for I did not know that I could be that bold and that courageous...!

FIFTEEN

A very small seed

You have within your hand a very small seed

It is so small that I alone can see it

But it is there I know

I am the One who placed it there when I created you

Open your hand and see it fall

Watch and see a hand coming down from heaven

And pick it up before it reaches the ground

It is the hand of God

It is the hand of the One who loves you

SIXTEEN

Fall of 1966

As I stepped outside the beautiful penthouse where I had lived an almost idyllic existence, my heart was heavy for I was now facing a very uncertain future. I missed my little friend who, a short while ago, had tragically perished at the hand of a careless driver. I missed her parents who had been so kind to me but above all, I missed Don who was busy guiding people to the summit of Mount Rainier.

My entire possessions consisted of two small suitcases, an old canvas backpack, a few photos, a French passport and an American tourist visa. It was not much but it was mine. It seemed that my destiny was to be a lone traveler on a lifelong pilgrimage, searching for the answers to life's questions, wanting to love and be loved at all cost and above all, seeking God and seeking a green card! I missed the many beloved books, mementos and treasures that I had left behind in France, but I had become an expert at traveling light!

Things had not changed much for as I stepped outside the beautiful penthouse, I was only holding two small suitcases and a backpack filled with a host of happy and sad memories. But was I destined to also be a traveler carrying a heavy heart?

September was fast approaching and Don would soon be back at Yale University. I had learned to accept his absences and his inability to help me for he was after all and above all, a college student facing a bright future and his priorities were to his studies. I loved him enough to wait and to keep him away from my never-ending immigration problems.

But at this moment, in time and in space, I was feeling very much alone, abandoned by life, by Don and by God! It seemed like I had finally run out of options for, as I said in the previous chapter, I no longer had the energy nor the willpower to look at the want ads in the New York Times as I had done a year ago... I may have felt fragile on the outside but in my heart, I counted on my grandfather's help from high above, now more than ever before!

I may have felt vulnerable on the outside but deep inside, I was still as strong as ever for the prayers I had heard and the wisdom of old that I had gained in my Ursuline Convent were not gone for they had been solid enough to shape my life and my heart. All the trials that I had gone through had tested my faith and made it literally impossible for me to now give up and get off the trail that God had laid out for Don and I.

I may have felt alone but I was not really alone!!!

So I chose, once again, to rise above my emotions, listen to the silent and yet very real heavenly voice within my heart and continue soaring, high above and across the clouds! I chose to stare at the tall and imposing building that was staring at me from across the street and I began to wonder and to dream. Would they have a job for me...?

I moved that night into the YWCA where as a young woman, alone in a big city, I thought I would be safe but no such luck for many of my French clothes were stolen on the very next day!

But it really did not matter for the last family I had worked for had given me an extraordinary amount of money before leaving the Hamptons, and Bloomingdale's was, after all, within walking distance from the YWCA! I moved within a few hours to a different and hopefully safer location!

Not knowing what to do, other than to go dress shopping, I decided to play "tourist" and pay a visit to the United Nations. I had lived across from this imposing and beautiful building for close to a year and it was high time to get acquainted! I was also wondering how I could penetrate this mighty fortress and get a job...

But if it meant being a tourist for a short hour, so be it!

Our guide, dressed in the exquisite apparel of her native South Korea, took us through the General

Assembly, the Security Council and many imposing and large rooms. She also kept us safely away from where I really wanted to go, but it really did not matter, for I was a very determined young lady and I promptly asked her where the personnel offices were located.

Receiving special clearance to enter the tall administration building was nothing short of a miracle. God must have been on my side for it looked as if the doors of this tall and imposing building were opening, one by one, before my very small eyes!

After taking the elevator to one of the top floors, I walked into a large office filled with people of all nationalities, tongues and colors and it felt as if I had just stepped into the tower of Babel!

After sitting for a few hours, my name was finally called out and I plainly and simply asked if they had a job for me! I may have appeared innocent and naïve on the outside but deep inside, I was more like David about to face Goliath and I had no intention of losing this battle.

I was no longer the shy and frightened young woman who had boarded a ship, in Le Havre, France and had landed four days later on what had looked like Ellis Island…!

I was no longer the shy and frightened young woman who had been unsure of her future and her destiny, after losing her old self to a brain injury.

I was slowly becoming a force to be reckoned with and I was beginning to feel good "dans ma peau*"!

I was asked to come back on the next day and take an exam in three separate languages! All the hours that I had spent studying English and Spanish had not been in vain and I was hoping and praying that I would be able to retrieve and bring back to life many of the French words I had forgotten!

My heart was leaping within me for I knew how extraordinary it was for me to take this exam which, twenty-four hours ago, I had not even planned on doing. I wanted to sing and dance but I had no one to share this moment with! And yet, I knew that, high above the clouds, my grandfather and the angels were doing a dance of their own!

As I sat before a desk the following morning, I could not help but wonder if my brain would be up to this new challenge! As I stared at pages and pages of intricate questions, I counted on God to watch over me and on the Holy Spirit to be by my side for I needed all the help I could get, at that very moment.

But I was sweating...!

Everything in me wanted to gain access to this mighty fortress where citizenship and green cards no longer mattered and where immigration officers would cease to exist!

* dans ma peau (French) : in my skin (English)

But lo and behold, I was told, on the next day, that I was one of only two people who had passed! Little did I know that God had saved me at the last hour! If I had waited one more day to visit the United Nations, I would have been unable to take this exam! The General Assembly was about to convene and I would have been too late and missed my opportunity to work there. I was one of the last two people who were offered a position and a chance to start working there a few weeks later.

I soon after moved into my first apartment on East 88th Street, which I shared with a chemistry grad student from Columbia University and felt as if I had overcome the world! I had been forewarned that my job would be stressful, but it did not matter very much for I was so happy and so very proud to finally be inside the United Nations! My job, within the General Assembly, gave me the opportunity to know many foreign dignitaries. I kept on being invited to an endless number of embassies' cocktails and receptions and kept on being driven around in long black limos! It was a glamorous world but it was also as dark and deadly as L'Alpe d'Huez had been! It would have been so easy to fall, for to these men, youth and beauty were of the highest value while they spent three joyful months away from their homeland and their wives!

The temptations were there but I chose to say "no" and be faithful to God and to Don!

Don had, by now, returned to Yale University but I

had decided to stop spending my weekends there and watch a bunch of spoiled and immature college students get drunk and find girls on weekends. This was not my idea of a fun and relaxing time! Don had always chosen to stay on the outside of these weekend bacchanals and as a result, he began to spend more and more time with me, in New York City. It was and still is a beautiful city, which we needed to discover and experience...

We began to find pleasure in simple things that did not cost much!

Other than kissing which was always a top priority on both of our radars, we started exploring the city! We discovered how much fun it was to go window shopping on Lexington Avenue, step into many of the beautiful art galleries on Madison Avenue and eat fresh croissants in Central Park on Sunday mornings... Life was finally as perfect and as idyllic as it could be...

But January was still looming in the distance and dangerously approaching us ever so slowly.

The General Assembly would soon come to an end and unless I found another position, I would have to leave the country by the end of January and fly back to France.

Once again, I was facing a very uncertain future but for the time being, I was in Don's arms and nothing else mattered...

SEVENTEEN

The real love story

As I said in the previous chapter, life was as good as we could make it to be for the time being, but January was still looming in the distance and yet, getting closer day by day! I had approximately six weeks left to figure out what to do and where to go next and I was now staring at the distinct possibility that I would have to go back to France. Going underground and becoming an illegal immigrant was an option that I had always categorically refused to consider! I was neither cut out to be a nanny nor to be an outlaw...!

My two suitcases and my canvas backpack had been put away, but it looked as if I might have to take them out in my near future!

Most of the people I knew, inside the United Nations, were foreigners and thus, were unable to help me. I now had the means to fly back to France but I did not have the heart to say goodbye to Don.

My parents were divorced and my father had since remarried and was living happily ever after, somewhere in time and in space. I had met his executive secretary, shortly before leaving for the

United States and I had known right away that this woman had always been after his name, his status and his fortune! Soon after, she acquired all three plus my father and a life of leisure for her and her two children. My father consequently chose to disown me and to steal from me what should have been legally mine including all my possessions, my books, my beautiful childhood porcelain doll and my inheritance.

It looked as if I had lost everything, but by falling in love with Don and coming to the United States, as difficult as it had been, I had gained a new life and had stepped into eternity. But this is another story...

My mother was continuing to spend countless hours on her psychiatrist's couch but seemed to be improving for she was now taking her medications and sounded almost normal when I talked to her on the phone which pleased me very much, for in spite of her illness and what she had done to me, I still loved her and had somehow managed to forgive her!!! How could I love Don as much as I did and still hold bitterness against someone else? Love and hate were never meant to cohabit in our hearts. One has to go...

Don's parents had never made any attempt to meet and know me for as far as they were concerned, I was a dangerous threat to the welfare and the success of their son's career! They had been opposed to our relationship from the time Don and I had met and they were fully intent on doing whatever they could to see me disappear. For some unknown and hidden reasons, his mom disliked French people as much as she disliked Catholics! I had derailed her plans to see him marry an Ivy League girl so as to have Ivy League grandbabies who, one day, would continue the family tradition and attend an Ivy League University!

Little did they know of my grandmother's aristocratic lineage and of my many ancestors who had been lords and knights! But I had chosen to keep this small but important detail hidden for my desire was for them to know me for who I was and not for whom my ancestors were. I, unfortunately, was never given that chance…!

His father was not only the President of the Yale Alumni Association but was also a renowned lawyer and held a high-ranking position in the United Nations Association. He was indeed a force to be reckoned with but so was I!

Time was no longer on our side for January was looming in our future. I needed a sponsor but we had been unable to find one! As a last resort, Don decided to ask his father to assist me in getting a visa. It would have been easy to do so for he was after all a lawyer, but his request was instantly and categorically denied!

Time had now become our biggest adversary and we needed to rapidly find a way to circumvent it!

As I said, we were young, immature, very much

in love and not always good at making rational decisions. Eloping seemed, at that time, the only solution that would allow me to stay permanently in the United States and little did we know that it would subsequently unleash hell in both of our lives and almost destroy our relationship!

The bride to be had to use a Webster Dictionary to find out what "eloping" meant!

To this day, I do not even remember what I wore on that day and what I said as we both stood in front of a Unitarian minister...!

I just wish I had been strong enough to say "no" and to choose instead to wait for God to move on my behalf, as He had done so many other times in my life. We had met on November 23rd, 1964 in Grenoble and we eloped on the very same date, two years later! Rather than being happy, excited and overjoyed, I was instead sad, very sad and so ashamed of what I had just done. My heart was telling me that I had just stepped into a world of lies and deceit and my emotions were telling me that this elopement had been the only way to stay with Don!

Two of my coworkers from the United Nations were our witnesses and to this day, I do not even remember their names and their faces!

Don left me early the next morning for he had to catch a train to Boston and then on to Rockport where he would be spending Thanksgiving with his grandmother, aunt and uncle as if nothing had ever happened. But it had!

I cried countless tears for I felt totally abandoned and alone, so very alone! I felt as if God had removed His presence from my heart and this, I could not stand! A part of me wanted to pack my two suitcases, my old canvas backpack, take an early flight back to France and try to forget that all of this had ever happened. But it had!

And yet, I still loved Don.

Was my love for him worth the amount of guilt and shame I was feeling now? In just a few short hours, I had become a person that I no longer recognized nor was proud of. Neither was God probably...!

And yet, I loved Don and so I stayed!

No one was to know what had happened on November 23rd, 1966 but the news somehow spread like wildfire, not only within the United Nations but also on the campus of Yale University!

We discovered a few years later that we might have been the inspiration behind the book and the movie Love Story! Its author had been Don's professor in a literature class and many on campus, including students, Masters of the Yale Colleges and Deans, knew of our own love story and elopement!

As required by law, I informed the United Nations of my change of status for I was still one of their employees and this unleashed a series of events that should have succeeded in destroying me but instead, were instrumental in helping me claw my way back to God!

Although Don's parents, the Immigration Services and the FBI kept on trying to bring me down, they could not.

Although they all kept on trying to separate us, they could not for God made sure that His own version of "Love Story" would prevail... Don and I were still its principal characters...

EIGHTEEN
Christmas 1966

As a woman now married to an American citizen, I was finally free to stay and free to get a job! But it was a sort of a pretend place to be in for I was neither a visitor nor a full-blown legal resident while I waited for my green card! But I did have my French passport and I held on to it with my dear life just in case... I should have been happy but I was not! I had never been good at lying and I was constantly afraid of spilling the beans. By eloping, I had stepped into a world of secrecy and pretenses, which I could not stand. I had always made my life an open book and I hated being a "closet bride!"

Christmas was fast approaching and Don would soon leave for Seattle where he would be spending the holidays as always with his family and try to act as if he had never eloped! But he had and I knew that these next two weeks would be extremely trying for him.

The General Assembly had ended and I kept on going back to the United Nations, hoping to find a job, but luck was no longer on my side, for there was none. If finding a temporary position at the UN had been almost too easy, I knew that I would need a miracle from high above to be hired on a permanent basis! These positions were of high value and required knowing the right people, playing games and manipulating the system, which neither I was willing nor had the energy and the time to do! My only recourse was to look, once again, at the dreaded want ads of the New York Times and try to find a job. Don could not help me and neither would my father for he had remarried and had now a family of his own.

I was a twenty-four year old young woman, alone in one of the largest cities in the world with no one to turn to and no one to ask for help.

God was silent and my heart was even more silent than He was...

Being fluent in French, English and Spanish proved to be very helpful in finding a job for I was still, after all, "married" to an American! I was hired, within a few days, by the French National Railroad where I started to work as a travel consultant. If I boarded imaginary trains on weekdays, I spent weekends with the many friends I had kept from the United Nations. It was a very eclectic and lively group of people and we all loved going to each other's homes and cooking exotic dishes, talking all night and trying to solve the world's problems or dancing the holidays away at the famed Club 54! Those were the days of mini dresses and tall and shiny vinyl white boots! I would be lying if I were to tell you that I did not enjoy being there. I did for I have always loved dancing!

I could have taken drugs for they were free flowing on the dance floors and I could have chosen to drown my sorrows in alcohol but I chose not to! I may have chosen to lie when I eloped but I had no intention to go farther down... and I was still determined to claw my way back up to God, one way or the other.

But it was Christmas Eve and I was feeling sorry for myself! Two long years had gone by and I was a long way from the mountains and the Alpine villages that were so beautifully decorated during the holidays. It was there that Don and I had fallen in love and yet, not a single time had we talked about God!

We had never spoken about the creator of these majestic mountains and glistening glaciers and yet, we had spent countless hours staring silently at His incredibly beautiful creation as we had both walked on snow covered roads.

If skiing and mountain climbing had brought him to the Alps , French existentialism had brought him to the University of Grenoble and these were still his "gods!" But I was young and in love! I had chosen to let my emotions take precedence over my spirit and let Don replace the God whom I had loved while growing up.

But as I sat in my living room, alone on Christmas Eve,

I was facing a long and dark night and I was not even sure, if I wanted to go to church or not! Attending midnight mass in a country that still felt foreign to me, listening to Christmas carols sung in English and sitting alone on a pew, surrounded by couples and families, would be a far cry from the wonderful moments I had spent, sitting in my grandparents' church and entering a magical and mystical world of its own! I was sad and wished to see this Christmas done and gone...!

My small job did not pay very much and I was barely making it financially. There would neither be a roasted turkey filled with chestnuts nor a decadent chocolate Yule log this year. I did not even know if I would be able to pay my next month's rent!

As I was watching television, trying to figure out whether I should go to church or not, the downstairs doorbell rang. Since I was not expecting any visitor, I looked through the curtains and saw a long black limousine parked in front of my building. I recognized the flag of the United Nations and promptly pushed the button to let my mysterious visitor in.

Three weeks had gone by since the end of my very short United Nations "career" and I could not help but stare in shock at the Ambassador of a French speaking African nation who was now standing in the middle of my small living room.

Over the past three months, we had become very good friends for although we had lived a world away from each other, we had much in common! His wife was French and had attended my convent school Saint Alyre! Our paths had never crossed for she was a few years older than me and yet, we may have sat next to each other in the chapel, totally unaware that our destinies would be linked one day. She was now married, lived hopefully a happy life in Africa and had several children. But my Ambassador friend knew that I had eloped for he was and had been a trusted friend for the past three months.

After chatting for a few minutes, he informed me that he had stopped by to say goodbye for he was on his way to the airport and would soon be on his way home. I knew him to be a Christian for he had always stood alone in the midst of a world filled with promiscuity, parties and drinking and he adored his French wife and his children! As he handed me an envelope filled with a large amount of cash, I froze and literally wanted to disappear for I really did not know what to say or what to do and yet, I desperately needed this money to pay my bills and potentially cover the cost of my flight back to France in January!

How would He have known unless God Himself had showed him to do so?

How would he have given me this envelope and insisted that I would never have to pay him back unless it had come straight from the heart of God?

He left the country that evening and I never saw him again. Once again, God had rescued me at the last hour, pulling me out of danger as He had done countless times in France and was doing now in this new country of mine...

But although I had been saved, I was feeling more like a war bride than anything else...

It was Christmas Eve, and I was alone!

NINETEEN

Call unto the heavens

Call unto the heavens
Call unto the deep
Call for the wind
Call for the breath of God
Open your hands
Lift up your arms
Look up to the sky
Open your eyes
Bend your ears
Stay still
Can't you see?
The heavens' door is opening
The deep is receding
The wind surrounds you
The heavenly breath is upon you
Wait a little longer
The breath of God is now your breath

TWENTY

A long walk on First Avenue

January had finally arrived! Don was now back on the East Coast and we had planned to spend the upcoming weekend together at my place.

I was still working for the French National Railroad and hoping to find a better job in the near future for being a travel agent had never been on my career path. I honestly missed the drama and the energy of the United Nations and I had felt more at ease with people of all nationalities and tongues than with Americans.

I was not really cut out to live in a dull urban world of brick and mortar buildings which bore no resemblance whatsoever to the world I had left behind... There was not much to admire outside my windows. It was a concrete jungle, filled with far too many people and far too many cars. It felt as if silence had simply vanished in thin air and as if people had lost the ability or the desire to stop long enough to look at the sky and hear the wind. It felt as if people had chosen to silence the voice of their own hearts. This vast city, which, I had chosen to live in, was cacophonous and bore no resemblance to the world I had so loved and left behind. Back then, I used to sit in wonder at the beauty of God's creation, listen to the wind twirling over the mountaintops. Silence had often been my companion of choice!

But my heart was now filled with sadness! The child in me wanted to escape and for a few moments, be like an eagle and soar over deep valleys, snow-capped mountains and glistening glaciers. But I was not a bird and I was no longer a child!

I was a young French woman who happened to have fallen in love with a tall handsome mountain guide in a land of enchantment and beauty. I had chosen to leave everything behind to follow my heart but I had also chosen to elope and lie for the sake of a stupid green card! I was married but not really!

I was living a borrowed life, which, I knew, sooner or later, would be discovered, and force me to take the steps that I did not want to take...

Spending Christmas alone had been an absolute bust for although, I had enjoyed being with my friends from the United Nations, it was not how I had wanted to spend the holidays. I may have felt like a war bride these past two weeks but I was also beginning to feel as if I were having an affair with the man I had eloped with!

But I was young and innocent, still loved Don and was unwilling to give him up!

I was utterly convinced that God had brought the two of us together for I was, after all, from the French Alps and he was from Seattle! It was a knowing that sometimes, did not make sense considering what I had gone through for the past several years... But in spite of what our lives looked like on the outside, I still knew that we were a life team, destined to stay together. Nothing would ever be able to break the cord that God Himself had tied around our hearts and our lives.

But the weekend had finally arrived and little did I know how far this assurance would be tested to its core in the next few hours, days and weeks to come... As I let Don in, I knew that something was different for instead of kissing and hugging as we always did, he somberly asked me to sit down and informed me that we were now divorced! I had not even had the time to get used to being married!

Don's parents had, of course, discovered that we had eloped and soon after arriving in Seattle, had left him no choice but to divorce me and within twenty-four hours, the no-contest papers had been filed in Kitsap County! But whether divorced or not, Don had stood his ground and informed his dad that he was still intending to marry me, the day after his college graduation which would take place two years from now!

In the meantime, I had become "a young and beautiful French divorcee" whose heart had just been broken and yet, was still in love with the man who had just divorced me...!

Don tried as hard as he could to help me understand why he had had no choice but to give in to his parents. His future at Yale University might now be safe and secure but my world had once again become very unsafe and very unsecure!

I was no longer certain of anything for I so wished he had called me before signing these papers. But he had not and it took me a long time to forgive him. I cried a thousand tears for I felt betrayed and yet, deep inside me, I almost welcomed what had happened for I could finally put an end to lies and pretenses. Everything was now out in the open and for this, I was thankful! At least, I could tell everyone that I was divorced and no longer lie about having eloped!

I had indeed been discovered for, within a week, I began to receive threatening phone calls at home and at work from the FBI and the Immigration Services!

Hell's fury had somehow been unleashed on my behalf! Someone had informed them not only of my elopement but also of my divorce and I had become a marked woman, facing deportation three weeks from now unless I left of my own accord!

I still remember the day two Immigration Officers walked into my office and ordered me to pack my bag and leave. As a divorcee, I was no longer allowed to hold a job in the United States and I had just stepped into a no-man's land! I had become a persona non grata but I still had a French passport in my possession just in case…!

It looked as if my powerful father-in-law had finally won but he had made a fatal mistake for I was not really alone in this strange and foreign land. The hosts of heaven surrounded me and my grandfather was on my side!

It had never been my intention to fight Don's parents, but I did not want to lose this battle, for I was not only fighting for my own survival but also for our relationship.

Although I had been deeply hurt by Don's decision to divorce me, we were still together and still loved each other deeply.

As I said before, I wanted Don to continue his studies at Yale University for I was convinced that he had a brilliant career ahead of him.

But I now had exactly three weeks left to find a permanent position at the United Nations. They were my only hope and I knew that I would need a big miracle from God to penetrate once again this tall fortress and make it a safe and permanent refuge!

So as I had done six months earlier, I wasted no time and once again, stepped into their personnel office… But there was no opening and the only position that would have matched my qualifications had just been offered to someone else… I felt as if I had reached the end of my rope and as if I were dangling on the side of a steep cliff!

To the eyes of the world, I was probably a naïve and somewhat innocent twenty-four year old divorcee, reaping the fruits of her lack of judgment and past mistakes.

I was now not only watched over by the FBI and the Immigration Gestapo but I had three weeks left to sublet my apartment and then fly back to France!

But to the eyes of God, I was a child in desperate need of His help...!

Saying goodbye to a land and a country that had made me feel so unwelcome would have been easy but I plainly and simply could not abandon Don after everything we had gone through. Two months had gone by and we had already been married, divorced and yet, we were still together!!!

I kept on reminding myself that God had brought us together and I knew, in my heart, that His plans would prevail but I just did not know how and when they would. I kept on reminding Him that the very real possibility of being deported was staring at me in the not so distant future... But He knew and did not need me to remind Him!

I was sobbing as I left the United Nations...

I was sobbing as I walked thirty-nine long uptown blocks on First Avenue...

I was still sobbing as I opened my mailbox and found

a long United Nations envelope addressed to my name...

Fifty some years have gone by but I have never forgotten this moment.

It felt as if a light from the heavens above had entered the room where I was now standing.

It felt as if a silent voice was encouraging me to open the envelope I was holding in my trembling hands. I did and yet, I was unable to read a single word for my tears blinded my eyes.

It felt as if a voice from high above the clouds was now reading for me...

There had indeed been an opening at the United Nations.

There had been one perfect job and I was the one to whom the position had been offered! I will never know nor understand how this happened but God knew and once again, had rescued me at the very last hour! My tears were no longer of sorrow. They were tears of joy and thanksgiving. My heart was dancing before the One who had loved me enough to stretch out His hand and manipulate the United Nations system!

I knew then more than ever that God wanted the two of us to be together and that our love would prevail.

My enemies had permanently lost for after signing

a new contract, I became an employee of the United Nations and came under their protection.

Neither the FBI nor the Immigration Services could ever touch me again and enforce my deportation. I soon after stopped receiving threatening phone calls and Don's parents disappeared from my radar.

I had not really won this last battle! God had...

TWENTY-ONE

My short United Nations Career

As I started my job, I felt elated for I would no longer have to fight the Immigration Services. God had won and He had placed me under the legal covering of the United Nations. I knew that He had moved heaven and earth to make this position available at His perfect time!

Being a trainee proofreader was far from easy for my eyes had to withstand spending countless hours reading pages and pages of countless documents! I worked in the French Section but sharing our large office, were also the English and the Spanish teams. Everyone's job was to fix grammatical and typographic errors as well as to make sure that all translations were correct. I was young, inexperienced and would have to slowly work my way up to reach my coworkers' level of excellence. They were all brilliant and over time, they became my heroes!

The Russian Section was located across the hall, away from all of us. We were still in the middle of the Cold War and they pretty much kept to themselves.

But a friendly Russian interpreter started to talk to me whenever we rode the elevator together. We were soon having lunch together in the cafeteria for I knew he loved France but I am not sure the French language was the only thing he was interested in...! But as intuitive as I was, I somehow knew that we were being watched! This went on for a few months but came abruptly to a stop when I discovered that my phone had been tapped! Soon after, he was forbidden to speak to me. Who thought that I may have been or was on my way to become a spy? Was it the French, the Americans or the Russians? I'll never know, but so much for my short career as a double agent...!

I loved my new job for it was a world of international intrigues and high drama.

Nothing and no one was ordinary!

These were the days of Apartheid in South Africa, the days of the Cold War and as such, commanded a high level of emotional, moral and political drama that permeated all the documents we were reading day after day.

Although Don and I still saw each other every weekend, we were having a hard time adjusting to being divorced and we had not quite recovered from the recent storms we had weathered together. Those were difficult, uncertain and painful days but as we had done when we first met, we chose to talk and lay everything out in the open. This had always been my way of choice to look at the messes I had got myself in throughout my life and to find the best way out!

We were still very much in love, living on a part-time basis as a married couple and yet, we were divorced...!

Don was now spending long weekends in New York and I rarely set foot on the Yale campus, unless forced to. In spite of our elopement, our divorce and our weekends spent together in Manhattan, he kept on maintaining honors-level work for he was indeed brilliant.

He left the East Coast in early June to go on a 10-week expedition in the Yukon Territories. Although most of the people he would be climbing with were highly professional mountaineers, I was greatly worried about the qualifications of the few who had chosen to come along and who were far from being experienced climbers!

I knew that he would be facing many risks, especially from deadly avalanches but I had to trust that God would watch over him and shield him from harm. Quite a number of climbers actually lost their lives, that summer, on Mount McKinley and elsewhere in Alaska while he and his team were climbing Mount Logan! But Don reached the summit and left there one of my purple French scarves!

The summer had been long and trying for I had had

no way of knowing if he was still alive or dead but Don had finally come back safely from his 10 week-long expedition and had returned to Yale University to start his junior year. Our peaceful existence resumed but it was about to be threatened by a new set of virulent attacks coming from Don's parents.

Having by now an international and permanent visa from the United Nations, I was beyond their reach and there was not a thing they could do to force me to leave the country. But Don was about to become their next victim or prey!

He was, once again, served an ultimatum, which made him stronger than ever for they had not counted on their son's determination to finish college and marry me the day after his college graduation. In fact, he had made up his mind long ago in the French Alps! In a few short, cold and unloving words, his parents chose to withdraw their support and required him to cover the entire cost of his Yale room, board and tuition which was, even then, an exorbitant amount of money!

They were hoping that he would finally come to his senses and leave me once for all.

The tides had turned and he was now the one who would have to fight not only for his survival but also for our survival. But I knew that as God had been on my side, He would also be on my ex-husband's side! I knew that soon or later, Don would let go of his existentialist idols and meet the One who was about to cross the heavens, stretch out His hand and help him.

He started to work as a consultant for a clinical chemical company while being a full-time student, a fellow in the Chemistry Department and maintaining excellent grades!

Instead of going back to Seattle and working as a guide at Mount Rainier, he chose to stay close to me and away from the life he had known and from the parents who had just deserted him.

He also held on to a night job at a nearby factory and worked as a forklift operator to the amazement and the amusement of his coworkers who could not understand why they had a Yalie in their midst...!

Just as he had spent most of his young life climbing high and sometimes treacherous mountains, he was now more than ever determined to succeed and reach the summit, which to him, was our wedding!

He worked non-stop to the amazement of his roommates, friends and professors and he worked non-stop to the consternation of his parents.

He held three jobs, kept up with his classes, managed to cover his entire senior year, have extra cash, head for medical school and be admitted to Harvard, Stanford and Mc Gill!!!

Although I was proud of what he had accomplished in the midst of trying and painful circumstances, I was mostly proud of whom he had become.

I may have fallen in love with a tall and handsome mountain climber, five years younger than me in the French Alps but I had now, standing by my side, a man whom I could trust to be my companion for the rest of eternity.

I had not made a mistake when I had fallen in love, way back in Grenoble.

To my eyes, Don will always be, the tall and handsome mountain climber who captured my heart, way back in Grenoble but he had now become so much more, so infinitely more...

TWENTY-TWO

Don's Grandmother

In spite of all the dangers and horrific moments that I have had to traverse throughout my life, I never doubted that God was there!

In spite of my stubborn streak, God had always been patient enough to wait and see whether I would choose to continue going my own way or finally decide to place my hand into His and go His way!

Have I always known that God loved me? Yes!

Have I always felt loved? No!

I certainly did not on June 10th 1969 and yet, I should have for as we both stood before a Catholic priest, I knew that this second marriage was nothing short than a miracle and that I owed it all to God! But I had no tears left to cry whether of joy or of sadness!

Sitting behind me were the people who had so cruelly, time after time, tried to destroy me and yet, had miserably failed for God had chosen to rescue me and save me from their wrath.

Sitting behind me were the people who had so obstinately tried to kill our relationship and yet, had miserably failed for long ago, God Himself had tied our lives and our hearts together.

But also sitting behind me, was Don's grandmother who had shown me nothing but kindness from the first time I had met her. She was a remarkable woman and to this day, she has remained as close to my heart as my own grandparents were.

Although she had been born in Metz, France, she was of Swiss descent but had been raised in New York City where she had lived a life of great privilege and affluence. And yet, she had suffered greatly for her mother had committed suicide!

We had much in common, for we both shared a deep love for France, its culture, its language and its food! She was a true breath of fresh air for she gave both of us love, acceptance and encouragement in the midst of utter disdain and disapproval. She knew of our story and yet, she had chosen to love us in spite of or maybe because of it! We had both suffered much and in spite of the fact we were now legally married, we were still carrying many scars that would take a very long time to heal!

Don had chosen Harvard Medical School and we were now living in Cambridge, Massachusetts where we would be spending the next five years of our lives for my husband had chosen to take an extra year doing research. He had graduated Magna Cum Laude from

Yale University with a double major in French and Chemistry and these two subjects were to keep on waging war within him for the rest of his life! French had his heart but his brain loved science...!

I had not "graduated" from the United Nations but I had succeeded in obtaining a green card by arguing my case before the Immigration Services. Having been awarded a permanent visa from the United Nations made it illogical to seek a sponsor since I was legally employed and they had had to succumb to this rational reasoning and I had won!

I had finally become a legal resident in the United States and I could have probably embarked on a successful career within the United Nations and become an editor in the years to come but this was not to be my destiny and I walked away from it all.

I chose to follow my heart and follow Don to Cambridge, Massachusetts!

I was, once again, living in the city that I had been forced to leave four years earlier but God, somehow, gave me the ability and the grace to forget it all and go on with my life!

Our first apartment may have been small in size but to us, it was nothing short of paradise for it was truly ours and we knew that we had not only conquered our enemies but also the curse of the Love Story tale!

Don's schedule was horrendous and kept on increasing in intensity and severity as the months went by for he had to divide his days and nights between medical and surgical rotations, finding time to study and working part-time as a computer programmer at the Massachusetts General Hospital!

I was at first working as a patient advocate in one of the local hospitals and then, as the Director of the Foreign Languages Department at Cardinal Cushing High School in South Boston.

As it had been in the French Alps, we still loved the outdoors although there were no longer any mountains in our fields of vision! But Don's grandmother lived in a beautiful house, located in Rockport, on the rocky North shore and we loved spending our weekends there. I also think she loved having us stay with her!

She was indeed an extraordinary woman who had chosen to fly to France in the midst of the First World War where she had worked as a translator and a Red Cross nurse. It was there that she had fallen in love with a handsome wounded American Officer whom she married soon after coming back to the United States!

We both loved to listen to her many adventurous tales and watch her come to life when she recounted her own love story! We both looked forward to playing Rummy in her kitchen alcove until the wee hours of the morning and she seemed to always look forward to our visits!

Although she was not really my grandmother, I felt often as if she were for we had a real and deep affection for one another. She loved gardening as much as my little Franciscan grandfather had and she spent a great deal of her time caring for her beloved flowers.

God knew that I loved her and honored who she was and I truly believe that He brought her back to us many years later. We were at the time living in the suburbs of Washington, D.C. and great was our surprise and our delight when we learned that she had chosen to stay with us for two long weeks before flying back to Seattle where she now lived. Her health had deteriorated but her heart was still full of love and her intellect was as bright as it had ever been. We spent two long and precious weeks reminiscing over both of our lives as if we were two old friends and realizing how much we had in common in spite of our age differences. Although she had never before talked openly about her faith in God, she began to do so and I discovered how she had always loved God and had tried to serve Him as faithfully as she could. She had been and was still an amazing woman of God!

As we said goodbye to her one final Sunday evening, I could see big tears falling down her face for she and I somehow knew that we would never see each other again. I knew that she was about to walk back into a difficult situation but God delivered her and took her home early the next morning!

She walked straight through the doors of heaven and met there, my little Franciscan grandfather who, probably, could not wait to show her his new rose garden!!!

Her beautiful house on a rocky shore has now been sold but the memories of the wonderful times we spent there are as vivid as ever in my memory and I look forward to seeing her again one day.

TWENTY-THREE

A French Southern Yankee

The five years we spent in Cambridge had been difficult but not insurmountable for we knew that nothing or no one could ever again bring us down or separate us... We had approached Harvard Medical School, as one more summit to climb and neither one of us had been afraid of this new challenge! Our lives, so far, had been nothing short of adventurous and I had an inner sense that it would continue to be so! Our lives had been far from being ordinary but we were as much of a team now as we had ever been in the French Alps and in New York City! God had tied our hearts and our lives together and neither a harried schedule nor a lack of money had been able to pull us apart.

We had joined a local "hippie" co-op and this had been my first introduction to the Woodstock flower generation where people loved one another, loved humanity and loved "green grass"! Don and I had chosen to bypass the green stuff and stick to the organic produce that we shared weekly among several families on our block. Although poor, we ate well and almost became vegetarian for it was infinitely cheaper to eat brown rice, tofu and eggs than to eat steak tartare! I now had to cruise the aisles of the local Goodwill store to find clothes for us.

I had chosen to bring my mother to the United States a few years earlier and to take her side in court so as to protect her from my father's wrath. She was no longer the person she used to be for she had chosen to go back to school and was now working as a nurse assistant in one of the local hospitals. She was on medications and once in a while, would have a few setbacks but somehow, would always manage to bounce back. Her patients loved her great sense of humor, her French accent and her beautiful smile. God had given me back my mother not as she had been but as He had made her to be and for this, I was ever so grateful to Him!

Having babies while attending Harvard Medical School was a rarity but in spite of it all, our first son was born in 1971, followed soon after by our first daughter. If we had been known at Yale as the "Love Story" couple, we were now known, at Harvard, as the couple who kept on having babies...! I had grown up surrounded by a host of nannies whose entire task had been to care for me and not teach me how to care for others! Don's parents had chosen to hide the fact that we now had children but miraculously enough, had been willing to cover the cost of medical school tuition and yet, stay uninvolved in our lives. My mother was busy working but she was kind enough to help us financially whenever a need would arise. My husband's grandmother supported us totally and she loved having our little ones stay in her house. We were young but we had a paperback version of Doctor Spock's book on how to raise babies, toddlers and children and we followed his advice to the letter as if his words came straight from the mouth of God! We kept on messing up but we kept on going, hoping and trying to be better parents than ours had been!

Don, as always, had excelled in his studies and managed to somehow graduate Magna Cum Laude with high honors from Harvard Medical School! As he stepped forward to receive his diploma, he was proudly holding his baby daughter in his arms as if to show the world and his parents, that he was so much more than a young doctor, he was also a daddy. If I had not cried at my wedding, I now did cry for I was so proud of him and so proud to be his wife and the mother of his children.

Once again, we had beaten the odds and although strained, our marriage was still in one piece.

I should have received a degree with high honors for having held the ship together for five long years of medical school, without having had a penny in our bank account but God had been faithful and had watched over us in spite of my now indifference toward Him!!!

If existentialism had been and was still Don's religion

of choice, medicine and science had joined the club and they would continue to fight for first place in his heart for pretty much the rest of his life. If he had graduated Magna Cum Laude from Yale University, with a double major in Chemistry and French, these two subjects were still waging war, five years later! French had his heart but his brain loved science!

Since moving to Cambridge, I had stopped attending mass for I had felt alienated in the contemporary English-speaking Catholic churches. As time had gone by, I had simply and sadly drifted away...

I was a wife and the mother of two very young children who needed me and neither did I have the time nor the energy to seek God and find Him! My lack of sleep had rendered my spiritual vision blurred and my ears were now solely tuned to my babies' cries! And yet, God was there as He had always been, waiting patiently for me to run back into His open arms, for He was still calling me back... But this is another chapter and I do not want to jump the gun...

Soon after graduating from Harvard Medical School, we moved to Durham, North Carolina where Don would be starting a yearlong internship at Duke Medical Center. As we drove south in a rented U-Haul truck, I could not help but become more and more anxious as I kept on seeing boiled peanuts and pecan logs being advertised on billboards. What were boiled peanuts...? As I looked at the Durham skyline, I started crying for there was only one "short" building rising in the distance...!

The year was 1974 and I was about to enter the world of June Cleaver where some women still wore bouffant and sprayed hairdos with great pride. Wearing black was a no-no unless you happened to be on your way to a funeral! I felt as if I had just stepped inside one of Tennessee Williams' books where women were still wearing candy colored dresses, white gloves, matching shoes and purses!

It was a world filled with unspoken prejudices and where I heard the "n" word for the first time in my life! I felt as if I had stepped into a Southern twilight zone and I honestly hated it.

I felt alienated for I had a hard time understanding everyone and neither could they understand me! I hated fried chicken, despised fried okra, could barely stand fried catfish and fried hushpuppies and never understood why anyone would eat fried ice cream! Where was Julia Child when I needed her?

I felt alienated from everything and everyone I had ever known and loved. Don was by now extremely busy and had basically disappeared from our lives. I had become a single mother, having to learn to make it alone in the midst of a foreign country where people spoke a language that I had a hard time understanding! Don's rotation schedule was much more difficult than the one he had just finished doing at Harvard for Duke took great pride in making their interns' lives as painful as they could and would later be commonly known as a marriage graveyard!

My husband was on call five nights out of seven, which meant that he only slept two nights out of seven and as a result, stayed for twelve months in a perpetual state of utter exhaustion! Since we only had one car, I would often have to wake up the children in the middle on the night and drive to the nearest hospital where I would sometimes spend an hour waiting for Don to finish a late admission, complete his charts and finally be able to take everyone home.

Money was very scarce for we only received a kind of stipend from Duke, which was far from being enough to meet our needs, but, as it had been in Cambridge, we never lacked anything. I had learned over the past five years to be satisfied with far less than what I had grown up with.

Although I still loved Don with my whole heart, I missed him terribly and I simply wanted him to come home and stay home but whether I liked it or not, I had married a doctor and his career would stand between the two of us for the rest of our lives. He was never really home for whenever we managed to be together, our times would always be interrupted by Duke calling him back to the hospital!

By the end of his internship, he had become a stranger to his children and seeing my daughter scream when Don would try to hold her in his arms, was very sad indeed.

I knew that the countless days and nights we had had to spend alone, away from one another, had wreaked havoc on our relationship. I knew that my husband's ingrained desire to succeed and become the best was slowly but surely eroding at his heart. We still loved each other but we were now facing an enemy much bigger and much more ferocious that we had ever had to confront. This enemy was firmly intent on destroying us, pulling us apart and obliterating God's plan for our lives and our marriage.

But as I had not given up in New York City, I was still not willing to give up on us!

If it meant fighting for our survival, I was willing to do it once again.

If medicine and academic achievements had been my biggest competitors for Don's heart, they were now also some of the tools that God used to touch my heart and bring me back to Him!

They were also God's choices to turn on the light within Don's heart and reveal Himself to Him.

If the combination of five years of medical school and one year of internship had been harrowing, we had never doubted that we would not make it. We had entered Harvard and Duke as a team and we were still a team as we were just about to embark on a new path.

This sheer determination is what had led me to slowly understand that our lives were no longer to be accepted as a series of continuous adventurous climbs but as a journey, which God Himself had ordained long ago!

Medicine, science and French would continue to wage a fierce war in Don's heart for a few more years but I never stopped hoping and believing that, one day, God would conquer his heart, his career and his life.

TWENTY-FOUR

A French idiot

Rather than going to Vietnam and fight a war to which he was opposed, Don had chosen to spend the next four years in the Public Health Service, and continue his research on brain chemistry at the famed National Institutes of Health!

As a result, we had left our rented apartment in Durham and were now living in Rockville, Maryland. His internship had finally ended but Duke Hospital had somehow wreaked great havoc on our relationship and our lives. Don was now a stranger to his children and I felt sometimes as if he was no longer the man I had fallen in love with in the midst of my beautiful French Alps. I felt as if our love had been surely and steadily eroded by a never-ending succession of medical rotations, one more difficult than the other.

Little did I know that I would have to compete for many years to come, with the enticing and highly addictive world of academic research, which my husband dearly and honestly loved! It was a perfect match for his deeply ingrained desires to help patients, to succeed and to become famous. If he was not working in his lab, he was at home reading scientific papers or writing grant proposals. My competition was not another woman, but a host of lab mice and various critters from the animal kingdom.

To our youngest daughter's eyes, my husband was a "rat doctor" as she once called him, when asked what her father did!

I knew that he still loved me but he ALSO loved medicine and science! I loved him deeply but it was no longer enough to hold our marriage together. We needed help!

God was there and yet, He was utterly silent.

He was there but we had become too self-absorbed and too busy to notice His presence and His never-ending offers to help us!

He was there but we had had chosen not to see Him!

But as always, He was far from being finished with us and He was still willing to give us as many chances as it would take to have both of us turn back to Him! The storms that we had barely weathered were the very instruments God would use to touch our lives and our hearts.

Our four-year-old son was fluent in French but severely lacking in his English language skills and for this reason, we chose to enroll him in a nearby nursery school, affiliated with a large Southern

Baptist church. As I should have known, there was only one spot left available!

Being French and having been raised in a Catholic school, I was highly suspicious of anything or anyone called Protestant. I had been taught that this western religion was nothing more than a cult but for my son's sake, I chose to lay aside my suspicions as long as I stayed away from this church sanctuary!

What did "Southern Baptist" mean anyway?

As weeks went by, we began reciting at home the short prayers that my son had memorized in his nursery school and my refrigerator was now covered with religious artwork!

For him and for him alone, we chose to visit the church that I had been so wary about. I literally thought that by stepping inside, I would sooner or later be excommunicated, but we both knew that we needed help from high above and we wanted our children to be raised in a Christian environment.

I knew that Don had attended an Episcopal church in his distant past but so far, had refused to convert to Catholicism.

What was the Episcopal Church anyway?

But since we needed help, not only as a family but also as a couple, I chose to shove down my suspicions, keep quiet, attend a local Southern Baptist Church and meet a new set of natives!

Everybody was super friendly but as a French woman who had always religiously guarded her privacy, I was neither ready nor willing to divulge my life story before perfect strangers, as nice as they all were!

I expected everyone to kneel down but no such luck for there was no bench to be found.

I expected everyone to close their eyes and enjoy a few minutes of silence before the beginning of whatever would come next but no such luck for everyone behaved as if they were at the mall!

I felt on that day and in the weeks to come as if I had stepped into a religious twilight zone. I was trying as hard as I could to join in but I simply could not for my heart was not in it! And yet, we kept on going back not only for our sake but also for the sake of our children, and God used our naive obedience to bless us beyond our wildest dreams.

Everyone carried a bible but how could I have one since I did not even know what this book looked like and was very much ignorant of its content, except for what I had managed to learn and retain from catechism classes!

My husband, on the contrary owned one, but it had been left untouched and unopened throughout our married lives. Its main function had been to gather dust and be a bookend!

Having an inquisitive mind and wanting to know what all these Baptists were raving about, I chose, one early morning, to give this book a try...! Without knowing where to start and for the first time in my entire life, I opened my husband's bible, and my eyes fell on the upper left corner of the page where two small lines literally jumped off and went straight for my heart!

"Do not hinder the children from coming to Me..."

My heart felt as if it had been pierced and I knew that I had been given an order to lay aside my fears and my many prejudices and obey the One who had spoken these words. It was not an exhortation! It was a command that I had no choice but to obey whether I liked it or not. I loved my children and the command had come directly from across the clouds. God was no longer silent in my life and had just ordered me to do something that I would have neither wanted nor been able to do on my own...

I did obey and I kept on attending this foreign Baptist church for I knew better than to say no to God! I wish I could tell you that saying yes had made things easy. It had not for I often felt like a total idiot on Sundays!

I was still very unfamiliar with the Baptist terminology and often wished I had had a religious dictionary of some kind to help me understand whatever these dear and kind people were talking about! Hopefully, they had a clue but I did not...!

I finally bought my first Bible but I spent most of my time in the table of contents. Praying aloud in front of others was nothing more than frightening for the only prayers I knew were Catholic and memorized. I also knew better than to recite "Hail Mary full of grace..." in front of these people!

Being Catholic, I was definitely considered lost! The tides had turned and were no longer in my favor for I was now on the other side of the Atlantic Ocean and a world away from my Ursuline convent! Most of the people were kindhearted but they had their radar on me and were fully intent on seeing me repent of my sins, be saved and dunked in their baptismal pool... As I said, the road was difficult and sometimes painful for as time went by, rather than seeing God's light and God's interpretation of things, I became more and more confused. But I had said yes to God's command and I was not about to retrieve my word.

I knew that I had loved God from an early age and that Jesus had died for my sins. I had been baptized and confirmed by a Bishop and did not quite understand why I was being asked to negate my past and be saved! I saw my life as a continuous series of moments and steps, which, if I chose to go in that direction, would ultimately lead me into His saving grace and, overtime, transform my life and my heart. I simply could not and would not believe in a "once and for all times" decision.

This created a lot of uneasiness and unrest in my heart, which I did not welcome. I was torn between what I had heard and been taught in France and what I was hearing now. I was not looking for another set of doctrines and another religion and I felt as if the territories where I was now walking were totally and utterly uncharted.

There was a particular Baptist ritual that I was still very uneasy about, namely walking forward to receive Jesus! I came from a land where the affairs of the heart had always been kept quiet and private and not advertised before hundreds of people! Listening to an open invitation at the end of each Sunday service would always make me feel awkward and uneasy.

As the pastor finished speaking on that particular Sunday, I heard a deep, loud and strong voice, resounding and bouncing across the entire sanctuary. Nothing like that had ever happened to me and I looked around to see if anybody else had heard what had seemed to come from high above.

God had ordered me to attend this church through two lines of scriptures jumping off the pages of a bible, but I knew instinctively now that I was being ordered to step out of the pew and to walk forward in front of hundreds of strangers...

Three times did I hear the command "WALK!!!"

Three times did I answer, in the stillness of my now cold heart, "No... over my dead body, will I walk..."

Three times did I choose to disobey for I was still a French woman and French people do not step out of the pews and walk forward in front of hundreds of strangers.

As I left the sanctuary that fateful Sunday, everything around me turned black and I felt utterly alienated from the God I had ever known and loved. The words that I had spoken and the steps that I had refused to take had plunged me into a deep and dark abyss. I felt totally alone, in a state of shock and wondering how I could have been such an idiot, a French idiot?

Would God ever give me another chance?

TWENTY-FIVE

The red shoes

The words that I had uttered and the steps that I had stupidly refused to take had plunged me into a dark abyss of some kind... I felt, for the first time in my life, totally alienated and separated from God and from His love. For some idiotic reason, I had chosen to say "no" to the One who had loved me from the beginning of time, and my heart felt as if it had been broken into a thousand pieces.

Would I ever see His hand coming across the clouds and reaching mine and would I ever hear His voice again? The only thing I could see right now was my stupid old self and the only voice I could hear was my own!

This call from high above had never been about signing my name on a so-called Baptist roster but it had had everything to do with my willingness to obey and trust God enough to place my life, my heart and my future into His hands.

Twenty-four hours had gone by but I was determined, one way or another, to fix my problem and to climb my way, once again, up to the heavens above.

So I chose, on the very next evening, to drive to an unfamiliar location and attend, of all things, an evening prayer meeting, which my Sunday school teacher had invited me to...!

As I drove in the dark of winter on snowy and almost impassable roads, I was not afraid for I was truly willing to do just about anything to let God know that I was finally willing to say "yes" and step out of the pew of His choice if He still wanted me to do so! But I was also hoping to find a few familiar faces once I got to my place of destination...!

No such luck for I did not know anyone and my so-called Sunday school teacher never showed up!

Once again, as it had been countless times throughout my entire life, I was surrounded by a new set of strangers and I had to endure the same kind of penetrating and invasive questions. They were trying their best to make me feel welcome but it was not really working. I was after all the only French woman who had just begun to get acquainted with the big book, and who still did not know how to pray in front of other people! This evening had all the promises of being "different" for these women were the leaders of a very large non-denominational bible study, which had just taken off in Bethesda, Maryland. Could someone please tell me what the word "non-denominational" meant? Where was my religion dictionary when I needed it?

Many of these women were the wives of senators and congressmen and I often felt small, inadequate and inexperienced. They were religious leaders and I was not! I had not even joined the club yet! They knew how to pray beautiful and "unmemorized" prayers and I did not! They knew every chapter, every line of every version of the big book and I was barely acquainted with its table of contents...!

Not knowing what to do and afraid to sound stupid, I chose pretty much to be a silent observer. A visiting missionary from South Africa gave a pep talk on the Holy Spirit and the "content" of her message was so good that I listened to her every word and wished, for the first time in my life, that I had had a pen and a notebook!

But as the women started to pray soon after, the beauty and the power behind each of their words floored me. It felt as if they went straight to the throne of God and straight to His heart! Deep within me arose an almost visceral urge to be like these women and to pray as they prayed.

My upbringing in my convent had formed my early spiritual life and had given me an invaluable foundation for these nuns had truly loved God, Jesus and the Holy Spirit with their whole hearts. My grandfather had been a spiritual force to be reckoned with and I was still reaping the influence and the benefits of his prayers on my life.

But I was now seeing that I was still a child when it came to the things of God and that somehow, I had just been placed among women who I wanted to emulate and catch up with...!

Their prayers and their words were spoken in a new language, which, until that moment, I had never known to exist, and which, I could not understand. Some sentences were translated and others were not!

Being French to the core, I could not help but notice a pair of exquisite red shoes, which the woman, sitting across the room, was wearing. These did not come from Payless but had Bloomingdale's or Nordstrom written all over!

While listening to the mysterious words that were spoken around me, and while staring at the shoes across the room, I began to realize that I could no longer move my head! I felt as if I had been transformed into a pillar of stone and as if I were now destined to stare at a pair of red shoes for the rest of my earthly life. I could still breathe but I could no longer speak nor move!

Soon after, a bright light entered the room and kept on floating and hovering around me. You need to understand that I was still a good young Catholic woman who had never experienced anything like this and who did not even know that one could see a light whose perfection was not of this world! No words could adequately describe the energy it seemed to possess and its beauty mesmerized the artist that I still was!

This light was iridescent, vibrant and full of an energy that I had never experienced before. Many years have gone by and my words are still too insufficient and too inadequate to describe this mysterious light that seemed to have come from a distant world and was now hovering over my frozen old self! And yet, I can still see it as if it were yesterday!

This light had come from high above, from high across the clouds and it was now enveloping me as if I had become an infant in an unearthly womb! I felt safe and yet, I somehow knew that I was slowly and methodically being emptied. All the hurts and the pain that I had endured throughout my life were now like puffed clouds, one by one vanishing and disappearing into the unknown.

But the extraordinary thing was that, as I kept on being emptied, I also kept on being filled by waves upon waves of love.

For the first time in my life, I knew, to the deepest core of my being, that I was loved and that I would keep on being loved! I knew that eternity had somehow become mine and that I had been given the second chance that I had so desperately cried for.

I had no scripture to substantiate, explain or rebuke what had just happened but I knew that God had looked at my heart and had sovereignly done what He had chosen to do.

This extraordinary light had touched a heart that had been broken and shattered countless times...

This unearthly light had healed the heart of a young woman who, at times, had felt as if she had died emotionally and spiritually and had contemplated suicide in L'Alpe d'Huez!

The heavenly light left soon after and I was, once again, able to talk and move around but I kept on being silent and being still for what had just happened to me was utterly unbelievable and needed to be treasured and not shared with anyone. How would I be able to explain it anyway...?

I knew that my life was no longer my own and that my heart was now completely His!

I vowed to never let go of the magnificent love I had just experienced and I never did! I vowed to follow Him and make my destiny His!

With tears running down my face, I ran to the front of the church sanctuary the following Sunday.

I was not signing my name on a new denominational roster. I was simply being obedient to the route that God seemed to have chosen for me.

I was alone at the altar on that particular Sunday, but not really, for I knew that I was surrounded by a myriad of smiling angels!

I could almost hear my Franciscan grandfather say "finally!"

I wanted to dance before the One who had loved me enough to send His light across the clouds and heal my broken heart.

Two weeks later, my husband and I were baptized together on Valentine's Day, but this is another story and another chapter...

TWENTY-SIX

The B.I.B.L.E.

Three weeks had gone by since I had refused to yield to God's command to step out of the pew and walk forward in front of a Southern Baptist crowd and yet, I had been given a second chance for my heart was no longer broken!

Stepping inside a Protestant church was not where I would have naturally chosen to go, as I had done a few months ago, but it had simply been the first of many obedient steps I would nevertheless have to take for the rest of my life.

Walking forward, as I had done two weeks ago, had been nothing short of a miracle. It was not what I would have chosen to do but I had had no choice but to obey and repeat somewhat reluctantly the pastor's words. I wish I had had the chance to speak words of my own but at that moment, in time and in space, it did not matter! My heart was and had always been His and it would continue to be so for the remainder of my earthly life. I was no longer my former self and yet, I was still the product of the faith of all my yesterdays.

Saying this pastor's prayer was so much more than the decision of a moment. It was part of a continuum which, years ago, I had embarked upon. I saw and had always understood that salvation was a process and a journey which would over time, transform me and enable to let Christ lead His life here on earth, in me and through me.

I had been baptized and sealed as an infant, confirmed as a young girl, but if this new and still unfamiliar Baptist religion, wanted to baptize me a second time, so be it.

Rather than celebrating Valentine's Day in one of the local restaurants, Don and I were on our way to church, on snowy and almost impassable roads. But we had an appointment with God and our new destiny, which we were not about to miss.

I had seen Don walk forward, a week ago for he had not wanted to be left behind and had chosen to follow me on this mysterious journey that I had now embarked upon.

We were about to celebrate our love for one another and our love for God by being dunked into an icy-cold water baptism pool! We had been forewarned that the malfunctioning heating system would cause the water temperature to be barely above freezing but in spite of it, we had chosen to go ahead and be baptized together on Valentine's Day! Little did we know that, in spite of our experience with snow and ice storms, we almost physically entered heaven together on that fateful evening! We survived but we lost the ability to speak for a few weeks.

Was God trying to test our willingness to obey Him or were we simply following the whims of a stubborn preacher who was intent on holding a baptism service, in the middle of a winter storm and on Valentine's Day? We may never know and the answer is no longer important...

Being "born again" proved to be a lot more difficult than I thought for in the depth of my heart, I was still as Catholic as I had ever been. I missed the beauty and the solemnity of my church's sacraments and thus chose to continue driving to the local parish where I would be able to receive communion! I had begun to lead a "double life" and was now forced to hide not only from the Catholics but also from the Baptists!

By being dunked into an icy-cold baptism pool, I had renewed my commitment to God but I was still questioning the validity and the necessity of my second baptism...

I desperately needed the help and counsel of a non-biased spiritual mentor but there was none to be found since everyone around me seemed to have been born Baptist! But the Holy Spirit began to help me understand the Bible for although I had attended French catechism classes and had listened to countless homilies, I was very unfamiliar with God's Word spoken and written in the English language:

I found attending Sunday School very frustrating for I was still learning to become fluent in this new Protestant jargon and to be able to figure out where the various books of the Bible were located. By the time I had located a passage of scripture, most people had already gone to another chapter, another verse and I was left, stranded in space and a foreign world of its own! My true salvation had become the table of contents!

I often felt like an idiot and if this was what a "spiritual babe" was all about, I was not enjoying it and wanted to grow up as soon as possible... I had landed into a nursery school of some kind where people kept on giving me their Baptist advice and kept on encouraging me to study more and to pray more!

I often felt as if I had stepped into an alternate world of some kind and yet, most of the people around me were super friendly, in an American and Southern kind of way! But I needed more than frequent potluck gatherings and weekly Sunday Schools to satisfy my hunger and the deep need to have an answer to the countless questions, which I still had.

Honestly! What was a French Catholic woman doing in the midst of an English-speaking Protestant Southern Baptist Church?

I was trying not to forget the language of the heart that I had always known and cherished since childhood as well as the mystical world that seemed to have always overshadowed me. Where were the great many saints of old who had been my constant companions while I grew up in France? I knew that they had not left me but I missed the mention of their names!

With the Holy Spirit's help, I was beginning to understand how important it was to have a deep knowledge of the scriptures but I was not prepared for the countless individual revelations that too many people seemed to have and to own... In the midst of this mess, I was also trying to reconcile my faith in an all-loving God with the message of hell and salvation that I kept on hearing from the pulpit, Sunday after Sunday! But as God had done so often, He not only saw the longings of my heart but He also heard my cries and chose to reach down from the heavens to help me.

Led by a force from above, I chose to go back to the women who had so beautifully prayed on a cold and snowy winter night!

I chose to go back to the place where I had seen God's healing light and where my broken heart had been mended!

I chose to go back to the spiritual giants who, for the next four years, took me under their wings and helped me not only to grow but also to soar.

It was the world where I found the answers to many of my questions and where I truly began to fall in love with God's Holy Scriptures.

It was the world where I met, week after week, women from all denominations who together chose to stand on the solid dogmas of the Christian faith and refuse to be distracted by denominational wordings, stubbornness, prejudices and religious pride!

It was the place where I began to understand that Christ was the "human face" of God, who I was in Him and who He was in me!

It was where I began to grow!

Within THREE years, I had finished studying the Gospel of John, the Pentateuch and quite a few Epistles but I was still unable to pronounce many of the names listed in the Old Testament!

Little did I know that my future would be linked with this worldwide ministry...!

If God's first call had been to step inside a Baptist church, my second call had been to step out of a Baptist pew which I had finally done after much reluctance on my part and a push from the heavens above!

If my third call had been to be dunked into a Baptist pool and to trust that God knew what He was doing, my next assignment would be to step, once again, into the unknown and bring what I had learned and experienced to North Carolina!

Although the task seemed overwhelming, I had learned better than to say "no!"

TWENTY-SEVEN

Prayer 101

The time had come for our family to pack and drive back to Durham, North Carolina, back to the land of boiled peanuts and fried ice cream!

My husband's stint in the Public Health had ended and neither Don nor I were looking forward to three long years of medical residency, a few added fellowships here and there and a year or two of research... Would it ever end and would I ever get my husband back? I was not sure that I ever would...

I was about to become, once again, a single mother of some kind and the children were about to pretty much lose their father! I was sad to leave behind the women who had been so instrumental in the healing of my heart and so influential in my spiritual growth. I honestly was not looking forward to being on my own!

Being obedient to God, seeing Him heal my heart and alter the course of my life and my destiny had been a life-changing experience. Digging into the Holy Scriptures had given me a deeper understanding of the Holy Trinity and how interwoven were the personhood of God the Father, God the Son and God the Holy Spirit as together, they danced throughout time and eternity.* Although I was about to face a great many lonely days and lonely nights, I knew that they would be there for me.

Because of their powerful and heavenly presence in my heart and my life, I knew that they would enable me to deal with my deep-rooted fear of abandonment and my unhealthy recourse to feeling sorry for myself! I still needed to let them weave their lives into mine!

Being a young medical resident's wife was far from being glamorous for I drove an old clunker, had very little money to live on and I was still cruising the aisles of the local goodwill store looking for thrifty bargains. Our house may have been small and our furniture used and abused, but it really did not matter for, in spite of Don's absences, I had somehow managed to fill its rooms with love, joy and laughter. I loved being a mom and my children were having the childhood that I had never had! If our home front was happy, my church life was still a never-ending source of frustration.

We had both chosen to walk away from fundamentalism for we had reached a place where we were neither able nor willing to continue listening to hell and fire messages. I was convinced that one did not enter heaven by being afraid of spending eternity in hell. It may have been a good sermon for some people but it was not for us.

*adapted from the writings of John of Damascus.

Attending a Presbyterian church seemed logical enough but without even knowing it, I had stepped onto John Calvin's home turf. As a woman, born and raised in France, I had been warned to never have anything to do with him and his theology. I felt quite uneasy about someone who had chosen to send his best friend, Michael Servetus and a few other folks to be slowly roasted for simply disagreeing with his doctrines. I was also beginning to realize that I myself would have probably been roasted if I had lived in those days! To the Protestants, I was a Catholic heretic and to the Catholics, I was an almost Protestant heretic for I had not quite decided whether I would or could accept the Sola Scriptura concept of things! No wonder why the world was having so many problems...!

If I was no longer surrounded by fundamentalists who had tried vehemently to figure out whether I had been saved or not, I was now a closet Catholic, trying to make it in the midst of friendly and loyal evangelicals, and a few hardcore, angry and not so nice Calvinists!

What did "being an evangelical" mean anyway...?

I had learned over time to bury my deep longings and my true beliefs and go along with the general status quo.

I had learned over time to stop dreaming and to stop wanting more for although attending and being involved in a church, was good, I had found my time spent there to be disturbingly unsatisfying and falling short of what my heart desired.

As young and inexperienced as I was, I somehow knew that I had been called to bring to North Carolina, the international bible study I had been involved with in Maryland.

The task seemed insurmountable for first, I knew very few people and second, I was still trying, with great difficulties, to understand and relate to Southern women who must have been formed from a different man than Adam...!

But as I had learned in Maryland, I knew better than to say no and walk away from this strange assignment, although everything in me was telling me not to do it...!

He had not called me because I could do it, but He had called me because as stubborn as I was, He knew that I would not go of this assignment until it was fully and totally completed.

I was still a single mother of some kind and fully responsible for the care and wellbeing of my little family but I began spending the next few months canvassing neighborhoods, churches and prayer groups and telling perfect strangers about this new bible study which was just about to burst on the North Carolina scene.

It was unlike me and unlike anything a French woman would had ever done and yet, I kept on going, full of a zeal that I did not even know I possessed.

I started asking women to come to my house once a week and over time, these meetings developed into a prayer group. I felt shy and out of sort, sitting in the midst of my own living room for I often felt very inadequate when someone would ask me to pray first! Why couldn't they let me pray last, for I would have at least been able to prepare my words but no such luck...!

Up to this time, my prayers had always been silent or memorized and they had all been spoken in French...!

All the books that I had read on "how to pray" had not helped much and I was as stuck as I had ever been. I had learned over time to cut corners and come up with all the rational and irrational reasons why I could not and should not accept becoming the new leader of this particular prayer group as I had just been asked... And yet, I could not refuse for I was the only person who knew about the Maryland study and I had a task not only to accomplish but also to finish...

God could not care less if I prayed in French or in English but these women did for they had not signed up for French 101!

And so, with a great deal of anxiety, fear and trembling, I said yes.

Why couldn't God have made it as easy as climbing mountains or skiing down pristine glaciers? But just in case, I came utterly prepared to each meeting with a brain full of carefully constructed and memorized prayers...! I felt more and more depressed as each week went by for I knew, deep inside that I was a fake.

Where was the French woman who had been fearless throughout her entire life?

Was I on my way to become someone I would not like very much nor be proud of for the rest of my days?

As it had been before, the choice was now mine... I could either continue to bring my carefully constructed and memorized prayers, to look and sound like everyone else or choose to dare believing in God's willingness to help me through the hurdle I was now facing and register for English prayer 101 with the Holy Spirit as my teacher.

God knew that my sheer resilience would be the force behind my unwillingness to let go of the assignment He had given me even if it killed me!

With time, I learned to pray in front of small and in front of very large crowds.

With time, I learned to abandon my beautifully constructed English prayers and with His help, soar across the clouds.

With time, I learned to trust Him enough to let go of my fears, one at a time, one situation at a time...

TWENTY-EIGHT

Laying hands on a dog

If bringing this new dynamic bible study to North Carolina had been in itself, nothing short than a miracle, it had also been at times, frustrating and quite difficult.

I had often felt as if I had entered another alternate universe and experienced, first hand, the law of "religious relativity!" I felt sometimes as if I had fallen into a "black hole" of some kind.

I did not need this...

It was also there that I had learned to step out in faith and dared to believe that I could pray in a language other than my own, in front of small groups and in front of large groups...!

It was there that I had learned to tame my Gaelic fiery temperament and my French impulse to walk away from conflicts and strong disagreements.

I did not need this...!

It was also there that I got hurt to the deepest core of my being by the very people, who, I thought, had been called to love one another.

Welcome to the religious and dysfunctional version of the Church!

Being in leadership had never been on my radar for I was perfectly happy in my little niche, being a wife and tending to the constant needs of three loving and rambunctious young children, one dog and one cat! I had never liked titles and yet, I was now known as the Associate Teaching Director and seen as the faith-filled "mascot" or good-luck charm who had brought this new study to North Carolina! But as I said countless times, I was not special! I had simply been obedient to God's calling....

My new position required me to oversee the care of all small group leaders and to spend a vast amount of time on the phone solving never-ending problems. But I did enjoy helping others and this would serve me well in the years to come!

Being the second-in-command required me to give an occasional lecture for which, I felt totally unprepared and inadequate. I had barely finished mastering the Bible's table of contents, was still stuttering mildly and spoke English with a strong "exotic" French accent which I knew some Southern folks would find difficult to understand! It was indeed a very awkward place to be in for I did not have an Aaron standing by my side. I was not Moses! But just as he did, I also had the Holy Spirit and I was firmly counting on His help! But just in case, I prepared and studied as hard and as much as I knew how!

Our household was facing a tragedy of its own for our beloved dog was dying and we all knew that he would not survive the upcoming night. My heart was utterly broken for he had been a loving and faithful friend and I was still not very good at saying good bye!

Ironically enough, or simply orchestrated from the heavens above, I was to teach on a particular passage of scriptures where Jesus had laid hands on the sick. But the only thing I could think of, for the moment, was my beloved Zipper who was slowly dying by my side. Parvo was and still is an almost always incurable canine disease and unbeknownst to us, our dog had caught it in the early months of his young life.

But as I kept on studying, I began to wonder why I could not do what Jesus Himself had done...

Why couldn't I lay hands on my very sick and very dying dog?

Why couldn't I do what Jesus had commanded us to do and continue doing?

Why couldn't I expect to see my dog well and healed?

I knew about "healing" for my two grandfathers had spent countless summers carrying paralytics into the cold and icy pool of Lourdes, in southern France but I lacked the time to figure out whether it was theologically correct or not to lay hands on a dog. I did not even know what to say or what to do but I loved "Zipper" enough to jump in, pray as Jesus prayed, leave the results up to Him and go to bed for I truly needed a good night rest before giving my first and ever so dreaded lecture.

Morning soon arrived and I heard the children yelling "Mom, come and see Zipper"! And so I did, stepped into our bathroom and stared in utter amazement at my dog who was very much alive as if he himself knew that he had been given a second chance!

I knew instantly that heaven and earth had met on that night!

As Jesus had laid hands on the sick, I had simply done what He had ordered all of us to do and continue doing.

As young and spiritually unsophisticated as I appeared to be, I really was not for I had dared to believe that the blessings and the promises of yesterday were not a thing of the past.

I had dared to believe that Christ had always been and still is our Healer!

As always, God had not only given me what I needed but He had also, first and foremost, given me WHO I had needed in my hour of desperation and despair! And yet, I was fully aware that divine healing was a large mystery that needed to be approached with great humility and a tender heart.

I was not as immature and spiritually unsophisticated as some people thought I was...!

But for the moment, my heart was filled with joy and gratitude and how could I not include this wonderful miracle in my lecture?

I DID!

All hell broke loose within a few days for I was subsequently required to appear before the pastor of the host church as well as a few deacons, face a modern day inquisition of some kind and ordered to recant my words in front of the entire class on the following week.

ONE DOES NOT LAY HANDS ON A DOG!

Alone, I had been judged and condemned for not a single person came to my defense or my help and offered to pray with me. I knew that I would never be asked to teach again but I did not really care for as far as I was concerned, my children were happy and our dog was alive and well!

Soon after, the national leadership asked me to become the area Director and oversee North Carolina as well as Eastern Tennessee and yet, the local leadership never allowed me to give another lecture!

I chose to resign later for the wounds I had suffered at the hands of these so-called religious leaders were too deep to allow me to stay. It would have been so easy to retreat into my shell, stay angry at others or blame God but I knew intrinsically that He had had absolutely nothing to do with what had happened and with what I had experienced.

It was my choice, as it had been before, throughout my life, not to let this unpleasant affair fester and to let God redeem it at His appointed time, in His chosen way and His manner!

It was my choice to let God put to good use what I had gone through so as to be prepared for what was lying ahead of me!

I chose the latter path and chose not to walk away from Him but to continue walking with Him!

Bringing this bible study to North Carolina carried a heavy price for not only had I been hurt at the hands of a few stubborn religious people, I had also experienced being shunned, being marked and being forgotten as if I had almost never existed! But it was also there, that I became stronger. My spiritual armor might now be dented and somewhat rusted but my warrior spirit was stronger than ever and ready for the upcoming battles that I knew I would face in my future!

Nothing is ever wasted if only, we choose to let God use it for our good...

The years that I spent in this study were a combination of happy and sad moments, of healthy and unhealthy relationships, which are a reflection of who we are and what our lives are...!

Why would we expect religious groups and churches to be functional when we, ourselves, are not?

I may have stepped in an alternate and southern religious universe, three years ago, but it was there that I had learned to love people whom I did not necessarily like and it would be a lesson that I would have to continue learning for the rest of my life.

It was there that I had learned to forgive and it would also be a lesson that I am still continuing to learn!

What if I had said no to God's call to bring this study to North Carolina?

Because of my obedience and my refusal to give up until the work was finished, countless lives and hearts had been and continue to be transformed, healed and renewed.

Knowing the cost that I paid, I would still do it...!

Our beloved dog wandered off to die many years later...

Several of our pets died of cancer in the years to come...

As I said, divine healing is a mystery for although

God is the author and the giver of life, He is also supremely in charge!

I may have walked through a "black hole" of some kind but I had survived!

TWENTY-NINE

One foot in each camp

Many years had gone by since I had stepped out of the pew and ran to the front of a Southern Baptist church! On that fateful day, I had not cared whether I had looked like a fool or not for God alone had mattered!

Many years had gone by since I had started getting acquainted with the Bible and rather than looking at it as a complex and intricate book, I considered it now to be my friend and my textbook.

Many years had gone by since I had left New York City and the United Nations. I was no longer living out of a suitcase and moving from one place to another and North Carolina was now my home!

I was no longer the person I used to be for I had gone through an intense and thorough immersion and I had slowly become the French version of a Southern woman as if these two very different entities could ever cohabit within me and become one...! But as people love saying, God works in mysterious and unfathomable ways...!

Don and I had joined a small Pentecostal church where we had found nothing but kindness, love and a simple faith. But because of the deep wounds I had suffered at the hand of a very few religious and intolerant people, I was at first reluctant to open my heart to others. I also knew that being angry and bitter was not an option, for in the long run, these feelings would wreak destruction on my emotions, my heart, my body and my relationship to God and others! It was infinitely easier said than done, for being on my guard and being in control were much safer than allowing myself to be emotionally vulnerable and thus, run the risk of being hurt again! I somehow knew that by closing my heart, I ran the risk of seeing it hardened and this, I would not and could not do for callousness and bitterness would make it impossible to give and to receive love from Don, the children, my friends and ultimately God Himself.

This, I could not and would not do for I wanted to continue being loved and being able to love others! I also had the constant prayers of my little Franciscan grandfather to help me for I knew that, not once, had he ever let go of me...!

So in spite of it all and because of it all, I kept on going! I kept on climbing my own stairway to the heavens, one step at a time, one day at a time, refusing to stop dreaming, refusing to stop wanting more of God and being utterly convinced that He would heal my broken heart at His appointed time, in His chosen manner.

I may have given a single lone lecture while attending this new bible study but ironically enough, I was now being asked to speak at various women retreats and to my greatest surprise, it was then and there that I discovered my true calling.

As an ex-stutterer and a French-bred woman, I absolutely loved standing behind a pulpit or in front of a blackboard and teaching women to pray and hear the voice of God! Every time I stood in front of an audience, my heart would be filled with a never-ending bubbling joy and gladness, gratitude and fulfillment for I had finally found my niche and it was in the midst of these precious moments that my heart began to mend. It was in loving these women, in praying with them and for them that I began to receive love from high above the clouds.

And yet, it was sometimes frustrating for in the midst of a weekend retreat, I often lacked the time to help them understand the language of the heart.

Although the memorized prayers of my childhood had certainly been helpful in my spiritual formation, they had often not been enough and from early on, I had learned to speak to God, as if He had been sitting next to me, as a friend, as the loving and ever-present father that I never had!

Although I had been so afraid to pray aloud in front of others, the Holy Spirit, not as an "it" but as the Third Person of the Trinity, had been there to lead me and teach me.

It was now my time to pass on to others what I had experienced and what I had learned. It was my passion, my drive and my joy!

I still remember vividly a particular Sunday that I spent in Sampson County. It was and still is a rural area where one can see endless serene tobacco and cotton fields and where women are always asked to "share" and not to preach! I had learned, over time, to accept this male status quo and not let this "southern and sexist" terminology affect me for whether a man or a woman, I knew that the Holy Spirit would do His thing, no matter what...! As I started to "share", on that particular Sunday morning, I soon enough realized that I would constantly be interrupted by the sound of flushing toilets for the men's and women's bathrooms were curiously enough, located on either side of the pulpit!

I could either cry, laugh or let the Holy Spirit take over and I chose the latter as He started to give me the ability to bypass the background noises and "preach" in spite of the constant flurries of activities behind me! He was in charge and I had simply become a conduit, a participant and a bystander as I saw Him shower people with bubbling joy and laughter, much to the discomfort of the local pastor and much to the delight of the people who were bold enough and needy enough to step into this river of pure, unadulterated and healing laughter! As always, I had never seen nor experienced anything like this but I knew enough, in my heart, to be still and let

Him move in the way and the manner He Himself had chosen! Many people were healed on that day...

As I said above, I had found my niche and I absolutely loved reminding people that, from the beginning of time, God has and is still speaking today! His nature has always been to speak but we, as the people of God, have often chosen to doubt our abilities to hear His voice!

Listen to the wind over the distant hills.

Listen to the crashing waves over the rocky shore and stare in wonder as the sun rising above the horizon.

Listen for a fleeting moment at the babbling brook cascading down the mountain.

Listen to the birds outside your window and the boisterous laughter of children and you will hear His voice.

Listen to the often silent and yet overwhelming voices of abused women, children and orphans and you will hear His cries!

As you choose to stay still and become silent, you will begin to hear the voice of your creator, rising above the waves, coming across valleys and mountaintops, piercing the highest and deepest clouds and ultimately, reaching your heart.

From the beginning of time, God spoke and He is still speaking today but our brain, our fears, our religiosity and our intellect have silenced our hearts and dulled our spiritual ears! Because of it, we have often missed noticing God's presence in our midst, missed hearing His voice and missed embracing His spirit!

So I kept on teaching, kept on reminding "hermeneutic" aficionados that God not only speaks in His Word but also in the liturgy of the Church, in the voices of the Saints of old, in the incredibly beautiful world that God gave us and in the hearts of His people!

Our call is not so much to ask but to be asked. Not so much to speak but to be spoken to. Not so much to love but to be loved. "Be still and know that I am God" became my passion, my teaching motto and my call to see people slow down, stop running and start listening to a heavenly heartbeat!

As I kept on teaching and speaking in front of small and large crowds, I also realized that God had healed my speech and my heart in the midst of His calling upon my life! And yet, in spite of the joy I was experiencing, a small part of my heart was still missing the liturgical church that I had known and loved while growing up in France but which was no longer the same since the Vatican II! And yet, I knew with certitude that I was where God had wanted me all along.

Would it ever make any sense and would the deep longings of my heart be ever satisfied?

In my heart, I still had one foot in the church of my youth, but I had also a foot firmly planted in the Pentecostal waters into which I had chosen, for the moment, to jump in and swim!

I was no longer a stranger in a strange land for I loved their passionate form of worship, their willingness to step on water when needed and their almost childish and yet powerful faith when they prayed!

I had finally found a faith-filled community, which I loved, and yet, I was still missing receiving communion and the Virgin Mary! Why couldn't there be a church body where the Holy sacraments would be combined with a deep respect of God's Holy Scriptures and the fiery Holy Ghost anointed prayers of Pentecostalism?

Would such things be ever found?

Would I ever find what my heart was looking for?

I felt often as if my life had been a long and strenuous climb!

I felt as if I were going from camp to camp, always striving for higher and higher altitudes with the Holy Spirit as my guide.

As it had been in the mountains of my youth, the journey had been at times painful and treacherous but at other times, it had also been glorious. I may have felt as if I had a foot in two very different camps, but my heart was at peace. Although I was still frustrated at times, my heart and my life were still His and I was in His camp!

Would I ever find what my heart was looking for?

Maybe and maybe not...

THIRTY

Being an artist

As I sat on the front porch of our mountain house and stared at an exquisite small rainbow that looked as if it had been supernaturally and magnificently placed between the two trees to my left, I could not help but wonder at God's incredible sense of humor, be in absolute awe of His immense and unique creativity and be reminded of His extravagant love! The rainbow lasted long enough to enable me to call my husband and as we both stared, him as a scientist and me as an artist, at this unique and exquisite supernatural wonder, we could not help but be filled with a renewed sense of hope and encouragement!

I have always loved rainbows for they are the perfect reflection of God's artistry and a perfect reminder of His promises and His faithfulness. To the French, they are an arc in the sky, "un arc en ciel." To the English, they are a rainbow. But whether in French or in English, whether an arc or a rainbow, they are multicolored gifts, sent from the heavens above, to encourage and fill us with hope and wonder.

Whether in the beautiful pink granite coast of Brittany or the magnificent snow-capped French Alps, I was surrounded by beauty from an early age and it formed in me the desire and the need to be free and not be in and stay stuck in a neat little religious box!

Being in the midst of these high and majestic mountains often made me feel very small for it was there that I had begun to understand how unfathomable and impossible to comprehend are God's power and God's majesty!

But it was also there, in the midst of energizing sunrises and glorious sunsets, that I had begun to love, cherish and need colors in my life. Being an artist made it impossible to live and stay in a neat black and white world.

I was the little girl who had loved copying the renowned French Impressionist painters.

I was the woman whose mind had been formed, at an early age, by the works of many French writers and poets and mysteriously enough, could recite many of La Fontaine's poems in spite of her brain injury.

Yet I was still, in an incomprehensible way, the little girl who had kneeled countless times before the statue of the Virgin Mary and the cross of Jesus.

I was still the child who had loved and admired her Franciscan grandfather and had prayed to God as her Father.

I was the product of my yesterdays and God had used them all to shape and form who I was now!

In spite of all the years I had spent in the very American and very Protestant church, I had found it difficult to forget the beautiful and mystical world I had left behind. It was still implanted in my very complex and multi-faceted memory bank! And yet, North Carolina was now my home for it was there that our children had grown up and where Don and I had built our lives together. We now had a small cabin in the Blue Ridge Mountains where we loved retreating to, every chance we got and where we reconnected to one another as mountain lovers, or should I be bold enough to say, almost "mountain worshippers"...!

I still loved my handsome mountain guide as much as I ever did and I still believed that God had supernaturally moved heaven and earth to bring us together and keep us together for it was not always easy being a doctor's wife. Although we no longer climbed high mountains together, we now hiked and loved being in the mountains of His Holiness, and being in the cathedral of His glory.

It might no longer be the land of edelweiss and blue gentians but it was the land of rhododendrons and exquisite flowers.

And no! Neither was I a tree hugger nor a nature worshipper, nor a flower child, nor did I smoke green grass...!

Although I escaped as often as I could to our beloved mountain house, I was now living in a world, filled with ladies' luncheons, bible studies, workshops and conferences.

Although I loved teaching, a small portion of my heart was still restless, frustrated and unfulfilled!

As I said in the previous chapter, I felt as if I had a foot in two very different camps.

I was an intuitive artist who saw God, the Bible and the world with the eyes and the heart of an artist.

I was also a highly analytical teacher who loved to open up scriptures, use her brain to present and expound God's Word before others but with the ever-constant help of the Holy Spirit.

From the Catholics, I had learned to value silence and stillness in worship, reverence and love the Sacraments. But the church of my youth had "evolved" and it was no longer what I had known it to be! As an artist, I had loved its mystical and mysterious aura, which had always filled my heart with peace and contentment!

From the Protestants, I had learned the value of self-discipline and diligence in studying God's Word and applying its principles to my daily life. As an artist, I had needed to place images on every page, every scene and every paragraph of the Bible!

As I said in the previous chapter, I had felt incredibly

and amazingly free among my dear Pentecostal brothers and sisters. It was there that my spirit had soared high above the clouds, and that my heart had danced before the lover of my soul.

I was neither Catholic, nor Presbyterian, nor Pentecostal when I preached and taught. I was simply His and yet, I had been formed and influenced by all the years that I had spent in these various denominations, But as I said above, no one had been able so far to put me, as an artist, into one of their neatly and carefully constructed black and white little boxes!

But it was this spiritual uneasiness and restlessness that God had used to have me keep seeking, keep on going higher and higher, always wanting more and always wanting to go deeper.

As I had done, while growing up in France, I kept on seeking the high meadows and kept on longing for the high places where one can hear the wind blow over mountaintops and deep valleys. I kept on wanting to go higher where the eagles soar, being firmly convinced that one day, I would find what my heart had been searching for!

But the meadows and the high places I was now seeking were of a spiritual nature and yet, they were filled with the images of my past!

I may have crossed deep crevasses and treacherous ravines along the way, but neither had I fallen nor had I been greatly injured.

It had all been worth it and I was still very much in love with the Lover of my soul!

I was still His and I knew that together, we would keep on climbing bigger and higher mountains...

THIRTY-ONE

The Swiss Cow

As a member of the Duke University team who had discovered the APOE Alzheimer gene, my husband was often asked to present a paper or a poster at many international scientific conferences. We both loved to travel across the world and we had become masters at combining work and pleasure. We especially enjoyed revisiting the places where I had grown up, meet strangers, eat delicious food and drink good wines in small and quaint cafes! I still remember vividly the day both of us chose to sing Amazing Grace, at the top of our lungs, in a magnificent and totally deserted French basilica! The acoustics were perfect and we felt as if we had reached Heaven's door. We were alone but we were not for I knew that all the saints who had worshipped in this church, for hundreds of years, were now surrounding us! Whether hiking or skiing in the mountains I had known and loved when growing up in France, or exploring faraway lands, we loved our lives and still enjoyed being together as much as when we had first met.

It had not always been a bed of roses but we had made it! We had chosen to never let go of the third rope that had so tightly been woven around us and had kept us safe in the midst of the many storms we had encountered. Rather than destroying us and pulling us apart, these storms had made us stronger and we were now, more than ever, a formidable team in the church as well as outside the church!

From the Baptists, we had learned to be unafraid and bold when talking to others about Jesus Christ.

From the Presbyterians, we had learned to apply ourselves to a careful and diligent study of the Scriptures, although John Calvin and I were still not the best buddies!

From the Pentecostals, we had learned to be passionate in our worship and our love for the Holy Spirit.

After all the years I had spent in the United States, I was still neither Catholic, nor Baptist, nor Presbyterian, nor Pentecostal and yet, in some mysterious ways, I was all of them for each had had a strong impact on my spiritual formation and I loved them all. I actually had a foot in ALL of these camps, contrary to the rigid theology of a few dogmatic church leaders, and I was still refusing to be locked up into one of their black and white denominational boxes!

Countless spiritual giants had had an everlasting influence on my life, my heart and my destiny. But I was still trying to reconcile, without much success, what I was seeing and experiencing in the American church with the church of my youth and what I had read and studied about the church of the Book of Acts.

I was neither able nor willing to accept that the days of miracles and healing had ended and that the days of dreams and visions had ceased to exist.

I also refused to believe that the days of wonder had disappeared into thin air when I had seen countless times the hand of God reaching across the clouds to heal, deliver and set people free.

Countless people now surrounded me, whether in conferences, retreats or ministries and yet, as an artist, I knew, that I would probably never fit in anywhere.

I still had many questions that needed to be answered within a non-judgmental atmosphere and as a woman, often lost and silenced in the midst of a patriarchal culture, I wanted my voice to be heard and acknowledged.

Little did I know that I would have to go back to the land of John Calvin, to the Swiss Alps to find the answers to many of my life questions!

Don and I had just finished spending a week in a beautiful Swiss resort, located on the shore of the Lake Leman and interestingly enough, straight across from the French village where I had spent many happy summers, during my early childhood.

Many of the Duke team as well as a few members of a large pharmaceutical company had congregated to strategize their next course of action and market their APOE discovery.

We had planned to leave at the end of the week and drive to Huemoz where the famous Christian ministry called l'Abri was located. I had devoured Francis Schaeffer's books and could not wait to get there and ask a few questions of my own, without being afraid of being labeled, condemned or sent to burn at the stake!

Soon after arriving, I discovered that we would have to sleep on bunk beds for there were really no accommodations for married couples since most visitors and interns were college students! Due to the exorbitant cost of electricity in Switzerland, people were only allowed to take one lone and single hot shower per week, risk hypothermia the rest of the time and were asked to work every afternoon, doing routine chores such as gardening, cleaning, doing laundry or folding everyone's socks and underwear! I would also have to attend daily morning lectures given by visiting Presbyterian ministers and theologians! I could either cry or laugh and I chose the former but it was not at all what I had envisioned. I was a long way from the five-star hotel, which we had just left, and yet, both of us knew that staying at l'Abri held an importance place in our spiritual journey for God had led us there and whether we liked it or not, we were not going to walk away and have a nice little vacation somewhere else! So we kept on telling the leaders, every evening, that we had decided to stay one more day and one more night and yet, trying to figure out why God would have us sleeping in bunk beds and working every afternoon during our EUROPEAN VACATION!

But we did adore driving high up in the mountains, each evening, and finding a quiet place to be by ourselves. As we sat there, we would listen and be enthralled by the exquisite and melodious sounds of hundreds of cowbells, which reverberated up from the meadows below and from the deep and mysterious valleys that lay before our eyes. These were our times to be silent, hold hands and let God speak to our hearts as we admired, with humility and gratitude, the incredibly beautiful world He had so lovingly given us.

These were our times to worship Him without the need of a spoken word or a single musical note!

As we sat, one morning, ready to listen to another intellectual lecture, I could not help but notice the relaxed and easygoing countenance of our speaker of the day. He was young and very learned. I could not help but devour each of his words and take multiple notes for he was describing the many struggles that his best friend had been forced to go through while navigating a host of denominations, always searching and yet, not quite fitting in any of them! His best friend was neither an iconographer nor a musician and yet, he was and had always been an artist, feeling at times alienated, rejected or misunderstood. He saw life and humanity through a different set of God-given goggles and spoke a language that most people refused to take the time to try to understand! And yet, he wanted his voice to be heard and his God-given talents to be recognized, valued and accepted!

As I stepped out of the room, I started crying for our speaker had plainly and simply described the second-half of my life within the American church!

As I sat alone on a bench, facing the mountains of my youth in the distance, with tears running down my face, I knew that I needed to take a good look at my life and try to connect the dots and find a measure of resolution if at all possible! I felt very much alone but God had already provided a well-fed Swiss cow to keep me company and make me laugh, for not once, did she walk away and let go of me...!

I was no longer French and yet, I was!

I was American and yet, I was not!

Would I be able and be willing to pick and choose the best of the two worlds that I had lived in and to leave behind what was no longer needed or necessary to hang on to?

As I had done multiple times throughout my life, I chose to begin to do so but also to run into His arms and ask Him to connect the dots of my life.

Only in Him, would my life become complete and made whole.

Later that week, we decided to embark on a late afternoon climb, on the French side of the lake and I will never forget what happened next as Don and I stood, on a very small and snowy mountaintop! We both saw a narrow beam of light, coming from afar, coming from the other side of the Lake Leman, coming across the water from Switzerland and now touching France. We both stopped in our tracks and stared in absolute wonder at this extraordinary and magnificent beam of light that ever so slowly reached us and showered us with millions of golden prisms. What we felt was totally irrational and totally extraordinary!

I felt like leaping and dancing, as I had wanted to do, hundreds of years ago, when I had stepped to the front of an unfamiliar Southern Baptist church but I could not for the ground under and around me was very treacherous and very slippery! God had chosen, once again, to reach across the clouds and show me His majesty and His power.

It was on the mountains of my youth that I found, once again, the God of the extraordinary, the God of the spectacular and the God who loved us enough to send us a beam of golden sunlight!

It was on the mountains of my youth that I understood that everything I had ever experienced from the time of my birth until now had been redeemed by God and would be used by Him to help me become His hands, His voice, His love and His light.

It was in the mountains of my youth that my heart continued to heal.

I began to understand that life was not and should never have been defined by my work and my so-called ministry but it had always been about Him loving me, about me responding to His love that I might in turn, love others. Countless times, had I failed the last part...

Would I ever feel again alienated, rejected and misunderstood?

Probably.

Would it hurt as much as it had on a few occasions?

Probably!

Would I ever stop having two feet in different and sometimes opposite camps?

Probably!

But for the moment I was enjoying this narrow beam of sunlight which had crossed a vast distance across the clouds and across a small portion of Switzerland and France to show me that God had everything under His control!

It was during our European vacation that I chose to walk away from teaching retreats and conferences and instead, concentrate on being His and being me...

THIRTY-TWO

Island of the Black Sheep

As I sat quietly in a very expensive and a very beautiful mahogany leather armchair, I could not help but wonder what I was doing in the midst of thirty male Methodist ministers...

As a woman and a fiery Pentecostal preacher and teacher, I was definitely out of my comfort zone and yet, I knew that God had orchestrated the somewhat awkward situation I was now finding myself in... If it had not been for the recommendations of several mainline ministers, who happened to be friends of mine, I would not have been able to take this "Inner Healing" workshop and penetrate this Southern Methodist "holy Mecca"...

As a French woman, I felt out of place but once again, my stubbornness and my refusal to give up were my biggest allies. I was there to learn and whether I liked it or not, I was going to stay! As a result, I chose to silence my emotions for the moment. I chose to bypass the fact that, as a woman called by God and yet, without a pulpit and a church, most of my answers, in the following days, were often ignored or viewed as emotional.

I truly believe that God has found and still finds great pleasure in placing me in impossible situations where I have no choice but to trust Him wholeheartedly and hope that He knows what He is doing! I also think that He is enjoying the ride! Up until now, my life had been far from being dull, far from being boring.

As I sat in a very expensive and very beautiful mahogany leather armchair, I knew that I would have to bypass my reservations, my hidden feelings of inadequacy and trust my minister friends to have known better when they had signed me up for this workshop! I knew that I was there, not only for myself but also to be better equipped to help others.

The length of time that I usually spent praying for people at the end of teaching workshops and conferences was far too short, far too limited. Divine healing had pretty much been relegated to the back burner of most local churches and laying hands on the sick had become a "touchy" subject of some sort!

As a Christian and as a French woman, I could not help but wonder why people weren't doing what they had been divinely called and divinely ordered to do.

My past had been broken and shattered to pieces countless times and yet, God had always reached across the clouds to touch my heart and make me whole.

How could I stay silent and not be the bearer of good news?

How could I choose not to tell others of His goodness and His love?

How could I refuse to pray for the sick and the wounded and not ask Jesus to intervene and touch their infirmities?

How could I stop believing that the God of yesterday was also the God of today and tomorrow?

I could not, for long ago, my life had stopped being my own!

This was the reason why I, as a woman and a Pentecostal preacher, had chosen to sit among thirty male Methodist ministers for a very long weekend! This was the reason why I had spent somewhat painful and frustrating two days listening to countless technical and intellectual data. Although informative, I knew it would not help me very much in the trenches, highways and byways of people's broken hearts and broken lives.

This was the reason why I was now sitting in the midst of a prayer circle, observing and watching what was going on around me and mostly, waiting for the Holy Spirit to make an entrance! I had chosen to be still, to be silent and to tell my brain to take a much-needed hike for it had worked overtime for the past two days.

A few minutes went by and I began to feel as if I had been gently transported into a world that was no longer my own.

I felt as if I was watching a movie reel being played before the eyes of my own heart and yet, as if the projector was located in the theater of my mind.

I felt as if I had become the little boy from the movie "Cinema Paradiso" whose eyes were full of wonder.

I had entered a world where images and words no longer needed to be understood through my finite mind but were plainly and simply revealed through the vast, mysterious and infinite expanse of my heart.

Out of all places God could have chosen, I found myself sitting with Jesus in a plain wooden rowboat! He was rowing and I was not...!

The sea around us had an almost crystalline and iridescent quality and I could not help but stare in wonder at its perfect beauty. But being still an analytical French woman, I could not help but ponder upon the ridiculousness of the situation I was finding myself in. There was absolutely no need for Jesus to row when He could have simply stepped out of the boat, walked on water, carried me or taken me by the hand to His destination of choice! But who was I to argue with the Son of God?

I soon noticed that the multiple glass floats, attached to our boat, were slowing us down considerably. As hard as Jesus rowed, we seemed to be unable to move forward and make any progress for there were simply too many floats.

Jesus proceeded to throw them overboard, ever so slowly and yet, with a great deal of force and precision. Each had a name and I saw my broken childhood, my tears, my sorrows and my fears being thrown overboard and being carried away by unseen dolphins and gentle creatures of the sea. I saw the deep pain, the rejection and the shame I had suffered at the hands of Don's parents slowly vanishing before my eyes. I began to understand why I had always felt different for I had stuttered most of my early life, had had thousands of French words obliterated from my memory bank after a tragic ski accident and had functioned as a woman called by God in the midst of a patriarchal, deeply prejudiced and obstinate religious world! I had experienced shunning and rejection but as I sat, in this small and simple wooden boat, I began to understand how these so-called floats had slowed me down and prevented me from becoming the person God had wanted me to be.

As my entire life was not only being exposed but also, being thrown overboard, our boat started to gain speed and yet, not a single word had been spoken between Jesus and me. He had kept on smiling as if throwing glass floats into a crystalline sea was and had always been His favorite pastime...!

We soon enough reached what appeared to be a deserted island but it was not, for as we approached its shore, I could see countless young and old black sheep playing in a very lush and very green meadow and running, galloping toward Him, toward us at the speed of light! As Jesus stepped out of the boat, He began rolling and playing in the grass, as if He were a black sheep Himself!

I could hear sounds of pure, unadulterated laughter and joy, coming not only from the island but also from the heavens above and I desperately wanted to step onto this magical land. Although it was totally and utterly out of my comfort zone, I knew that I had to get out of the boat and join the party, His party!

With Jesus by my side, I ran to the deep, lush and green meadow and began to jump and play with all the black sheep who seemed to be living there. I began to frolic among them as if I myself was a black sheep.

With Jesus by my side, I knew that I was loved and accepted even if I felt like a black sheep sometimes!

With Jesus by my side, I understood that although I had been born with a speech impediment, God had over time made me a public speaker. How could I not tell others of His gentle and yet, forceful love?

With Jesus by my side, I realized that although I had lost thousands of French words, God had chosen to make me fluent in another language and write this book. How could I not tell others of His unsurpassing healing power?

With Jesus by my side, I comprehended that I had indeed been different from others for I was, after all, a French "fish" who, at times, had been thrown into tanks of dubious and religious barracudas but God had always been there to protect me. I may have been bitten a few times but I had survived! How could I stay silent and not tell others of His goodness and mercy?

There probably would be many more times and many more occasions when and where I would, once again, feel like a black sheep for I was, after all, surrounded by sheep of all kinds and all colors, some nice and others not so nice! But I knew that I could always feel better and receive a much-needed healing by running, in the stillness of my heart, to a small island, situated in the middle of a crystalline and iridescent sea, where images and words were not meant to be understood through a finite mind but through the infinite expanse of a human heart.

I knew that I could always run to a small island, situated in the middle of a crystalline and iridescent sea, where Jesus, once again, would be waiting for me.

I knew that there was a place where I could be weak and yet become strong, where if I were ever lost, I would be found, where I could dare be vulnerable and yet be accepted, where I would always be assured that it was fine to feel like a black sheep sometimes...

After all, Jesus loved black sheep...

THIRTY-THREE

I came into being!

I view the days that I spent at l'Abri, in Switzerland as a gift from God! It gave me the chance to get away from my normal surroundings, reflect on the last few years of my life and cry many tears in front of a beautiful cow who was intent on seeing me through, for not once did she leave my side! I had found God long ago and yet, I felt totally lost for I had been unable, so far, to blend my artistic free-spirited nature with a somewhat rigid Protestant environment.

I had let myself become so busy that I had forgotten to keep a healthy balance between tending to my needs and the needs of others.

I had let myself become so busy that I had forgotten to take the time to rest and simply have fun!

Crying my heart out in front of a cow was not my idea of a European vacation but it had been, at least, highly "therapeutic" in a clean and healthy Swiss way!

Don and I had chosen, later that week, to drive to the small Alpine village of my childhood where I had spent many happy summers. It allowed me to reconnect to the little girl who had loved climbing many of the surrounding mountains and had always felt closer to God in a land, high above the clouds, where mountain goats are free to roam and flowers bloom. Being back in the small Alpine village of my childhood felt as if I was back home but I was not...!

To everyone living there, I was the girl who now spoke French with a terrible American accent!

To everyone living there, I was also the woman who had left the motherland to marry an American!

I was as much of an outsider here as I had sometimes felt in a small Southern town and living in the United States.

It had been infinitely easier to allow myself to be assimilated than to fight to keep my own identity. Over the years, I had allowed others to see me and accept me as one of theirs. Blending in had been far easier than standing out, but it had slowly and surely robbed me of my own identity and silenced the deep longings of my heart.

I was now living in a world where sacraments had been, to say the least, obliterated or pushed aside and yet, they had always been God's chosen way to enable me to reach up to the heavens.

They had always been God's chosen way to bring His Kingdom and His life into my heart.

And yet, I had kept quiet! But I could no longer be silent for the weeks that I had spent at l'Abri and the French alpine village of my youth had showed me that I could no longer ignore my yearnings. My desires were now too strong!

Being French, being an artist and being a fiery Pentecostal preacher would have somehow to blend, in the not so distant future hopefully, and enable me to fly and soar as the woman God had created me to be!

I may have been briefly swayed by the gods of existentialism while growing up but their cynicism and despair had driven me straight into the arms of God where I had found the answers I had been looking for!

I may have danced many nights away in dark and smoky discotheques and tasted of a world where people had lived like the devils and felt like gods but I had chosen to walk away from it all, feeling older and hopefully wiser!

I may have chosen to immerse myself slowly into a foreign religious culture where teaching, counseling and being the Director of a Christian ministry had become my identity. But I was now ready to walk away from it all and to reclaim the "real me."

I had allowed others to define me by what I did and not by who I was. And I no longer wanted to be asked what "I was up to" or "where I went to church!"

Being at l'Abri had been the catalyst behind my decision to walk away from all my religious activities, be still until I would hear, once again, the voice of God and feel His heartbeat and know His guidance! The phone no longer rang in our house and people had stopped dropping by... Our children were now in graduate schools and my husband, as predicted, had made several important scientific discoveries which kept him very busy, dividing his time between writing and submitting grants and traveling across the world to attend international conferences. I felt sometimes as if I was on the last line of his "to do" list! He had once told me that often, people "do" science for the wrong reasons...!

What were his true reasons for doing so? But this is another book...!

Silence now envelopped me and I chose to let it speak, for I do believe that it has a voice of its own. I knew that, one-day, God would call me back from a far distance and pierce the clouds that seemed to now surround me...

Would I be found and above all, would I find Him?!

Time had become my ally for it allowed me to take photography classes at the local Arts Council. It was a perfect match for I had found a place and a medium where my analytical, intuitive and emotional sides would hopefully blend nicely and where I would finally be able to let out of the grave what I had learned at the French Beaux Arts!

Soon after graduating, I was offered a full-time job at a pioneer Internet advertising company where I was forced to learn, not only on my own but also at the speed of light, how to use a Mac, a PC computer and Photoshop...! These were the worst of times for it was extremely difficult to master these new skills but they were also the best of times for I loved being surrounded by bold and daring individuals who stopped at nothing to reach their goals. They all wanted this company to be "bought out" at the highest possible price, retire as early as possible, buy a beachfront house in the Bahamas, drink countless margaritas and be surrounded by girls in skimpy bikinis...! I was back in the land of long ago and I could not help but wonder if I would pass the many tests that God seemed to have placed before me...

I may have left the barracuda tank but I was now surrounded by a much more dangerous and yet very attractive species of vertebrates!

I was now surrounded by many handsome young men who simply adored working with an older French woman and as a result, kept on asking me to go out for a beer or two or more...!

It reminded me of the days I had spent in L'Alpe d'Huez, but I was no longer the same person for I now lived in a different kingdom!

I would be dishonest if I told you that I was not flattered... I was!

I had one foot in the cookie jar and at times, I was tempted to put my other foot in...

Although Don loved me, he was also married to his career. The children had now a life of their own and many of my church friends had slowly but surely vanished beyond the horizon...!

In the eyes of these handsome young men, I was the perfect exotic French pigeon to be plucked for I was alone and lonely...!

I do not know why God had placed this job on the intricate, out of the ordinary and adventurous journey of my life but for the time being, I "was loving" it!

I had not truly laughed in a very long time and I had not had that much fun in an even longer time...!

Yes! I was tempted many times but not once, did I fall! My commitment to Don and our marriage was stronger than the enticing promises of young romances!

I was a married woman who was still very much in love with her husband for I knew that one day, hopefully in the not so far distant future, he would place me once again, first in his life!

I was also a photographer who took her job very seriously. Over time, I became very good at what I was doing, for not once, did I leave for a photo shoot without asking the Holy Spirit to be my eyes, my hands and to guide my decisions!

I may have been the oldest person in this particular office but I had an edge, for I made darn sure that each of my photos would be the product of a tight "working relationship" between the Holy Spirit and me. He was, after all, and had always been the supreme artist who knew infinitely more about light and darkness than I ever did!

He made me so "good" that I was asked to go to New York City to head another photography department.

He made me so "good" that I ended up being Director of Photography and having multiple freelance offers and shows.

From the moment I had joined this company, I had always wanted my photos to reflect God and the infinite beauty of His creation. I had always prayed that people would see Him through my work and that is why, He had made me so "good"!

As I kept on working there, handling one temptation at a time, one job at a time, I realized, one day, that my feet were no longer in different camps. They were in His camp, His boat and His ark with the extra blessing of having an "arc-en-ciel*" above, around, before and behind my head, my feet and my steps!

The various camps I had tried to live in, the best way I knew how, had somehow blended. I felt as if I had come full circle!

* arc-en-ciel (French) : rainbow (English)

I was a French woman, an artist and a now professional photographer who no longer preached from a pulpit and yet I did, for often, my actions preached louder than my words...!

I had finally reached a place in my life where I felt free to be me, swear at times, drink a beer or two with my husband and friends, talk to God in the midst of loud rock concerts and know that as an artist and a free-spirited human being, I no longer needed to be afraid of being me!

I had finally come into being...

The time that I spent working as a photographer in this young Internet Company will always make me smile for I truly believe that it was a gift from God, teaching me new skills, and putting into practice, in the deep jungles of life, what I had studied, taught and preached for years...

I was still a passionate and fiery Pentecostal preacher who happened to love liturgical services and holy sacraments.

I was a woman of God who happened to be a very good artist and felt now free to continue exploring and free to jump from one corner of His camp to another. For the camp was his Church and I no longer wanted to be labeled and relegated to being Protestant or Catholic or who knows what else...

I was a uniquely designed individual who happened to feel sometimes like a black sheep, but would, no matter what, continue climbing other mountains with God's blessing and God's covering.

I had finally come into being....

THIRTY-FOUR

The angel in a polyester suit

"People watching" is and has always been a French national pastime which almost everyone loves doing.

As you walk the streets of Paris or any other city in France, you will always find a group of people sitting outside neighborhood cafes, drinking strong and dark coffee, smoking cigarettes, discussing politics and sex, and commenting on the people walking by!!!

It is and has always been a national hobby!

I too have unfortunately inherited this Gallic vulnerability and I still catch myself, at times, looking at the way other women dress and judging them by their appearance.

I am well aware that my words and my thoughts reflect the condition of my spiritual heart, which is still far from being healthy and whole!

I am well aware that God is far from being pleased by my Gallic vulnerabilities!

I am well aware that He fully intends to expose them and send them into outer space.

If needed, He will choose to use unordinary circumstances to teach us very ordinary truths that will reveal and expose who we truly are!

How long can we really hide behind a fig leaf?

First of all, it is not big enough to cover many of us!

Second, God has and will most certainly continue to jealously and passionately pursue us.

Like idiots, we may think that we can hide the true condition of our hearts from ourselves and from others but we cannot hide from God. Sooner or later, we will have to either face open-heart surgery or circumcision!

As always, God was much more interested in my spiritual welfare than just watching me have a jolly good time while working as a professional photographer.

I had been asked to spend a few days in a small but ordinary Southern town and come back, hopefully, with hundreds of pictures, which would reflect its uniqueness. It was easier said than done for I was a French woman who used to have an intense dislike for anything associated with the South.

The days that I spent in this small but ordinary Southern town were actually delightful and I met a large number of superbly interesting characters whose portraits are now adorning the editorial walls of the company I used to work for!

I was scheduled, on that particular day, to take pictures of a huge farm where expensive and thoroughbred Arabian racehorses were being carefully raised before being shipped across the US and across the world. It was an extraordinary assignment, which, I knew, was of vital importance to my boss and my company. But I could not find a single person to help me with directions for this unique "farm" seemed to have been carefully and purposely hidden from the locals.

Out of desperation, I walked into City Hall, hoping to find there the help that I desperately needed for my job as well as my employer's reputation were on the line.

As I sat on an uncomfortable chair, while waiting for my turn to be called, I could not help but notice a woman who walked decisively toward a set of shelves. There, hundreds of maps were laid out, in orderly fashion as far as the City Hall employees were concerned, but in an undecipherable format as far as I was concerned!

I could not help but notice how remarkably beautiful she was BUT, she was wearing the strangest turquoise polyester suit that I had ever seen. She looked as if she had jumped straight out of a Sears catalogue from the fifties. We were in the nineties and yet, she was dressed as if she had just walked out of the television show Mayberry R.F.D.

BUT she was extraordinarily beautiful in a heavenly kind of way for her smile, radiant golden hair, demeanor and countenance stood out in the midst of an ordinary, busy and noisy administrative office.

After pulling a single map from the shelves, she walked toward me, stopped and asked,

"IS THIS THE MAP YOU NEED?"

Neither had we met nor spoken and yet, she had known exactly, at that single moment in time and in space what I had desperately needed for as I said above, my job and my employer's reputation were on the line!

I realized in utter amazement that the directions to the thoroughbred racehorse farm were clearly laid out and easy to follow. But as I looked up to thank her profusely, I realized that she had already left the room and as much as I tried to find her, in the next few minutes, I could not.

She seemed to have vanished in thin air in a mysterious and angelic kind of way! Somehow I knew, at that moment, that she was not and had never been of this world.

I knew that I would never be able to find her!

My conscience burned within me for I was very much aware that I had been found guilty of arrogance and pride before a heavenly grand jury! Even though this mysterious and yet beautiful woman had been sent from high above the clouds to help me and enable me to get to my appointment on time, I had judged her and condemned her by the way she had been dressed.

I had judged her as if I was still sitting in an outdoor French café, but I was not and I knew that what I had done was wrong. My Gallic vulnerabilities had been found to be in a great need of serious adjustments...!

This beautiful and mysterious woman had probably been my guardian angel sent from high above to help me and yet, the only thing that I had chosen to notice was her turquoise polyester suit!

Would I ever learn to stop judging people by their outward appearances and their demeanors?

Would I ever choose to zero-in on the inward qualities of their hearts and their lives?

Would I ever learn and choose to see the face of God as I looked at them?

Because of who I was at that time in my life, God had chosen this uncanny situation to teach me a valuable lesson which, years later, I am still learning to master and overcome!

An almost lifetime has gone by since that fateful day and God is still jealously after my heart, unwilling to share it with any Gallic vulnerabilities of mine!

As I said above, God will use extraordinary as well as ordinary situations to expose the hidden and yet destructive attitudes of our hearts.

Within a few months, I would once again, be helped by the forces from above.

It would no longer be about an angel in a turquoise polyester suit giving me a much-needed map.

It would be about an invisible hand steering my car away from oncoming traffic and thus, saving my life.

But this is, as always, the next story and the next chapter...

I just wish I had kept this map...!

THIRTY-FIVE

Lord, would you surprise Daniele!

I honestly do not think I would have become the person I am now if I had stayed in France! For as much as I love my native land and still admire its unique charm and beauty, I found it to be, in many ways, dark and depressing for its natives behave as if God had never existed! Being agnostic, atheist or existentialist was infinitely cooler than being a Christian. And yet, over the years, I have met in France, countless older God-fearing and God-loving individuals who are still bright and shining stars in the midst of a "dark hole!"

I still remember stepping, one late afternoon, inside the cathedral of Vézelay where for centuries past, hundreds of pilgrims had stopped there on their walking pilgrimage to Santiago de Compostela, in Northern Spain.

As Don and I stood there, we could not help but be mesmerized by some twenty Benedictine priests, all dressed in long white habits who worshipped God with their arms lifted up to the heavens and sang beautiful heartfelt Gregorian chants! As powerful as this experience was, I could not help but cry with joy for I knew that these God-fearing and God-loving monks were, once again, bright and shining stars in the midst of a "dark hole!"

Although I still felt alienated at times in the midst of western Protestantism, I had come to recognize that it was and had been God's chosen path to enlarge, circumcise my heart and align my mind, my thoughts and my will to His!

For the many years and the many people whose own path and spiritual journey had crossed mine, I will always be grateful! They were and had been God's chosen markers to show me the way and encourage me to continue my own journey...

I may have felt alone at times, but I never was!

I had always been surrounded by traveling companions, whether in visible or invisible forms, whose tasks had been to surround me, watch over me and show me the way.

Don, as always, was as busy as ever, seeing thousands of patients who did not seem to mind traveling or flying long distances so as to be seen by him. We ourselves divided our spare time between visiting the children who had moved on to other states, enjoying the peace and quiet of our mountain house or flying to exotic places where my husband could no longer be reached by phone! Attending medical conferences had allowed me to travel across the world but most of the time, I would end up being alone while Don presented a paper or a poster or a talk. I would, once in a while, get a glimpse of the man I had fallen in love with in the French Alps but these were fleeting moments. Let's be honest! I had married a handsome medical genius who loved me dearly but who also loved his career!

I was still working as a professional photographer and although I still loved my job, it had caused a lot of wear and tear on my body for I worked long hours and drove even longer distances between appointments.

As I left home one morning, to drive to our regional office, I still remember the words that jumped straight out of my heart, which catapulted me into a dimension where nothing, for the next few minutes, would be ordinary.

"Lord, my life is in your hands!"

Many years have gone by since this almost fatal car accident and I find it almost impossible to describe what happened next... My words feel as if they are glued to the page and unwilling to come out of hiding. As the images keep on popping out, fear threatens to swallow me and paralyze me, once again...

"Lord, my life is in your hands!"

Shortly after merging onto a busy highway, a speeding car forced me into the median where I began to spin uncontrollably. After facing the oncoming traffic on two wheels, I chose to jerk the car back into the median where still on two wheels, I knew, I would keep on spinning... I somehow ended up in my original lane where I faced another set of cars, which somehow, by the grace of God, managed to stop a few feet from me. All lanes had now come to a full stop and as people stumbled out of their cars, you could see the terror on everyone's face, including mine!

Not a single life was lost and not a single car was damaged!

I knew with certainty that an invisible hand and a stable Subaru Outback had combined to preserve, on that fateful morning, not only my own life but also other lives around me!

My world continued to be shaken in the following months as tragedies and illnesses kept on knocking on my door!

I discovered soon after recovering from a second kidney surgery, that my best friend's son had been killed in a tragic accident.

My brother had lost a long and courageous battle against brain cancer and because of the fragility of my health, I had not been able to fly back to France and see him one last time.

Soon after landing in Chicago O'Hare airport, I had learned that my oldest daughter, a few hours earlier, had lost her twin baby girls and my first grandchildren.

My beloved Persian cat had died at the hands of a voracious and hungry red hawk.

My short career as a professional photographer came to an abrupt end for I had torn my left biceps tendon and could no longer work long hours and carry heavy equipment.

My world had not simply been shaken. It felt, at that moment, as if it had died, as if it had exploded!

I had now joined the thousands of people who, over the years and at some time in their lives, had felt like Job! If death, pain, illnesses and tragedies had been the necessary requirements to join this club, I was more than qualified to become a member! I felt as if God had utterly and totally abandoned me and yet, in spite of my emotions, I knew deep down that He had certainly saved me from death, twice within a year, with the help of a stable Subaru Outback and the skillful hands of a world renowned kidney surgeon!

I may no longer be able to run for a while but my heart needed now to do the walking and lead me back into the heart of God! It may have felt as if He had abandoned me but He had not for He was still there, working in the background and waiting for the right moment to make His entrance on the stage of my ever so dramatic life.

People say that time heals but at this particular season of my life, it had not.

I had become afraid of driving on the left lanes of busy highways.

I had become afraid of answering the phone and hearing more bad news.

I had become afraid of facing a third kidney surgery and facing death itself.

I was especially afraid of the ever so familiar and ever so scary pain in my right lower abdomen which seemed to have popped up out nowhere, announcing the real possibility of a third surgery!

As I sat in church, on that particular Sunday, I could not wait for the service to end, walk to the altar and be prayed for. I was scheduled to go back to Duke Hospital on the next day and face another song and dance round of tests.

Knowing the gravity and the uncertainty of my medical condition, the pastor asked me to sit on a side bench while he prayed:

"Daniele, do you believe Jesus wants to heal you?"

I honestly used to! But as of that moment, I was plainly and simply paralyzed by fear and did not have the energy to believe anything or anybody!

"Daniele, do you believe that Jesus could surprise you?"

Probably yes! For I liked the uniqueness of this pastor's prayer and thus, chose to believe that somehow, somewhere and sometime in the far or not so distant future, Jesus would surprise me!

As I sat in a hospital room, on the next day, I seemed unable to forget about my upcoming surprise. Being a French analytical woman, I was trying to figure out where the surprise would come from and whether I would be able to recognize it or not!

As I lay on an icy cold table, going through a nuclear kidney scan, I could hear rumbling in the next room, which in itself was highly unusual. One of the radiologists came out a few seconds later and proceeded to ask a very peculiar question...

"Which kidney is healthy and which kidney was operated on?"

I was in one of the best medical centers in the nation but I began to wonder if I was in the right place! Weren't they the ones who were supposed to know for they had, after all, my entire medical and surgical records?

I was sent soon after to see my surgeon who kept on staring silently at the images of this latest scan as well as all the previous ones!

As Don and I sat, in the midst of this small and unimpressive examining room, there was utter and complete silence.

As Don and I sat on the edge of our chairs, we could not help but notice at how puzzled he looked.

Was this a good or a bad sign?

He kept on staring at all the images for quite a while, finally turned toward us and said...

"I AM TOTALLY SURPRISED and I do not know how this happened but there is nothing wrong with your kidney and you certainly do not need another surgery!"

Deep within my heart, I had just been given a surprise from high above!

Deep within my heart, I knew that a hand from heaven had reached across the clouds and touched my sick kidney.

Deep within my heart, Jesus had indeed surprised me.

THIRTY-SIX

You were my enemy

Yesterday
You were my enemy
The source of my pain
A constant reminder
Of a dark moment in my life

You were my enemy
The seat of my fears
The reason for my hiding

You were not of me
But you slowly took
A life of your own
Always to be feared
Always to be hidden

You took away much
But I also gave you too much

Today you are almost a friend
A source of hope
A constant reminder
Of a gift of a second chance

As I look at you
I see pride rising within me
For I did conquer the darkness
I did win the victory

As I look at you
I can be at rest
For I have now reached the other side

As I touch you
I see the gift that I received
I see healing in its wings

Because of you, I have life
Because of you, I can release the past
Because of you, I can rise and begin to
dream

I can open my eyes
And say yes to who I am and will be
And no longer grieve for who I was
All because of you

I may no longer run
But I am still able to walk
I may no longer win the race
But I have already received the prize

So today I choose to look at you
I choose to touch you

I choose to no longer see you as a
reminder of my pain
But as the instrument of my blessing

Today, you are no longer my enemy
Today you are almost a friend
Tomorrow, I hope to call you friend

P.S. This was written while recovering from my second kidney surgery. Because of it, I had been given the gift of life! And yet, I had been unable so far to look at a scar that was a constant reminder of the excruciating pain that I had had to go through. But as always, the Holy Spirit was not willing to let me stay where I was at and carried me high above into a sphere where I would begin to see things from His perspective!

THIRTY-SEVEN

you need to leave now

I am far from being a saint for my sinfulness and fiercely independent nature are always before me.

I was born in a far distant land, heard and spoke a different language and came to know God as a heavenly Father at an early age for as I said, many chapters ago, my father and mother had forsaken me and yet, the Lord had taken me in and placed me under His wings!

I have crossed many treacherous paths and climbed many high mountains over the course of my life and yet, because of His grace over me, I have managed to survive avalanches, deadly precipices and crevasses. I am now more convinced than ever that God has always watched over me, has always loved me passionately and extravagantly and is continuing to do so. I am His but He wants all of me and He continues to chip away at what is still not totally and utterly His.

I may have faced the forces of nature in the French Alps but little did I know that, out of all places, I would face many unforeseen and unfamiliar dangers in the small Southern town we had just moved to! I would face dark forces whose intent was, plainly and simply, to wipe me out from the face of the earth!

Such is the story, which I am about to share...

My husband had decided, once for all, to leave the gilded prison of academia behind and to embark on a new adventure! Duke Medical Center had been his world, his cocoon and his "golden handcuffs" for the past twenty-eight years and yet, he was eagerly looking forward to a slower pace of life which would enable us to spend more time together! How wrong could he be for the area we settled in was in desperate need of a neurologist of his caliber! Not only did he keep most of his old and faithful patients who would have been willing to follow him to the end of the earth, but he also gained countless new ones... His new practice grew at the speed of light and within a few months, he found himself as busy as ever. I found myself stranded in the foothills of the Blue Ridge Mountains, totally and utterly alone, away from my friends and the world I had known and grown accustomed to!

I cried a torrent of tears, yelled at God and felt totally and utterly abandoned by Him.

Although He was silent for the time being, He really was not. He was waiting....

As He brought local artists into my life, I began to make new friends and stop feeling sorry for myself!

Groaning and moaning were no longer my therapy of choice! I chose to look up to the heavens and accept the fact that my life had not ended. It would simply be different from what I had expected it to be...

The town we now lived in was quaint and pretty and yet, unsafe! Soon after our arrival, I was the victim of my first ever strong-arm robbery, which took place on Sunday afternoon in plain daylight and in the supposedly nice section of town!

Welcome to life in a small Southern town!

It was a land of pickup trucks, guns, hard-core Republicans and tea-party aficionados, good old bible-belt churches and cholesterol laden friendly cookouts!

In spite of my new artist friends, I knew I would have a hard time fitting in when someone admired the "costume" I was wearing while my husband and I cruised the aisles of the weekly farmer market!

And yet, in spite of it all, we loved this small town for it was exotic and very different from anything we had ever known! Music was an integral part of everyone's life and we truly enjoyed attending weekend festivals, mingling with the natives, learning the differences between bluegrass and mountain music and eating corn dogs...

It was the land that combined the genuine giftedness of Ralph Stanley and Eric Church and the earthly and unique humor of Sam Erwin!

To a woman, who had been raised in one of the most exclusive boarding establishments in France and had been required to curtsy when encountering a nun in the long hallways of her school, this new land was exotic in a new and foreign "Republican Hee Haw" kind of way.

Don and I decided to drive, early in June, to a nearby town so as to attend a new folk festival, listen to good music and eat totally unhealthy food.

Being who I am, I wanted to get a painted tattoo on my right arm. I knew that it was not permanent but while it lasted, it was as close to the real thing as I could ever get to.

Not only was it the land of pickup trucks and guns but it was also tattoo heaven!

Since we were supposed to attend a birthday party later that afternoon, we left early and walked back to our car, which was parked on a side street, behind the main stage.

The music was so loud that we had to cover our ears.

The street was utterly deserted, except for an older man, sitting in a wheel chair, on the front porch of his house.

A great sense of uneasiness came over me for I knew that something was not right for no one would be able to hear us or come to help us if anything happened.

If anybody had wanted to commit a crime, rob us or even kill us, it would have been the perfect place to do so.

Within a split second, I saw a young man approaching us slowly and cautiously.

I knew that he was up to no good!

To my horror, I saw him take out a small silver handgun out of his jean pocket, play with it as he slowly walked toward us, staring at me and staring at my eyes.

He looked as if he was trying to figure out how and when, he would take us both down.

The music was still blasting behind us and the man in his wheelchair looked totally oblivious to the drama that was slowly taking place before our eyes.

As far as we were both concerned, time had stopped.

To the world, we were alone and possibly facing a certain death.

To the heavens, we were now surrounded by a vast army who was intent on rescuing us from a possible death.

My husband grabbed my hand and we walked to the other side of the street, at a fast pace.

I looked back for a brief moment and saw the young man staring at us, still holding the small silver handgun in his right hand and yet, unable to move as if he had been transformed into a pillar of salt.

As we got back safely to our car, my husband said,

"I need to tell you something! While you were getting your tattoo, the Holy Spirit spoke to me and ordered me, three times, to LEAVE NOW! If I had been obedient, you would not have got your tattoo. We would have left early and would have probably never run into the young man with a gun."

How could I hold this against him when God Himself had chosen to intervene and protect our lives?

It was not the time to be bitter and angry.

As it had been in August 1942, I could not help but wonder why God had so blatantly, once again, chosen to save my life.

A lifetime has gone by and I still do not have the answers to why millions of people died during the Second World War and yet, I did not!

I still do not understand why so many people die at the hands of handguns and yet, I did not!

I may never know the answers nor understand the reasons why God allows some to die and others to be saved.

As I said, neither was I special nor am I special!

I just know that my life is a continuous saga of supernatural and sovereign moves of God's hand upon my life and my destiny.

THIRTY-EIGHT

The apricot poodle

Many years had gone by since I had given my last lecture and although I was enjoying my so-called retirement, my children and grandchildren, my two dogs and my roses, a part of me was still missing standing behind a pulpit and opening scriptures before others for once a teacher, always a teacher!!! Once called by God, always called by God!

Driving around our neighborhood in a shiny golf cart, playing golf and drinking cocktails were probably not in my future for my life's passion and desires were still to serve Him, be used by Him and see people come to know and experience Him in a more intimate way through my teaching. This was and had always been my drive and I would simply tell people that I was waiting for my next assignment when well meaning but irritating people would ask me what I was "up to!"

My hair may have been gray but I was still as much of an adventurer as I had ever been. My steps may have been slower but I had not stopped loving hiking on the Appalachian Trail...

I may have been the victim of three violent crimes over the last year and a half but I had survived each and every one. Overcoming tragedies and adversities seemed to have truly been my life destiny and yet, God had overshadowed and shielded my life each and every time! The last incident had been especially harrowing for someone had thrown a huge rock at the right side of our car and missed the windshield and my head by a few inches.

As I said in the previous chapter, we had moved to a small charming southern town and yet, a very dangerous one, for unemployment rates were sky high and drugs of all kinds were rampant. I should have died and yet, I had not! Honestly, why did God have to make my life so dramatic...?

I chose to forgive the hoodlums who had tried to wipe me from the face of this earth for if I did not, anger, fear and bitterness would take me over and ultimately bring me down. Why should I adopt the victim mentality since I had, after all, survived?

I chose to forgive these men for my own good and to do so, in the presence of a few friends for I needed them to be living reminders that I had said these words when tumultuous emotions and fearful memories would try to bring me down, in the days to come!

The healing process could have taken a very long time if I had chosen to take on the victim mentality but I did not, for I knew that the blood of my ancestors who had been lords and knights, would have boiled over if I had chosen to do so! Even as an adult, I still had needed quite a few prayers from my little Franciscan grandfather, which were safely stored in the prayer vaults of heavens above, but ready to be released on my behalf if needed!

I was asked to start another non-denominational bible study within a few months and since I had plenty of free time on my hands, I decided to do so. I chose to teach on the Holy Spirit and try to make people understand that He was simply not an "it" to be recognized on the Feast of Pentecost but that He was and had always been the Third Person of the Trinity.

But at the same time, there had been too much recent drama in our lives and Don and I felt that we needed a well-deserved mini vacation. Charleston seemed to be the perfect place to go to!

Little did I know, at the time, that two of our children would end up living in South Carolina!

I desperately needed to take long walks on the beach and breathe some fresh air...

I also needed to have fun, shop on King Street, visit top-notch art galleries and eat scrumptious food. To a French woman, Charleston meant sophistication, elegance, refined manners and the opportunity to finally wear my "so-called" costumes!

I was truly looking forward to spending a fun,

hopefully safe and peaceful weekend in the Holy City but to my greatest surprise, I kept on hearing, during one of my prayer times, that I would get a poodle in Charleston...! As always, it was a silent voice, rising up from the depths of my heart, which I had learned, over a lifetime, to recognize and take seriously! But this one was utterly ridiculous for I already had two dogs and did not need another four-legged critter to join our zoo! Being so blatantly analytical, my first reaction was to try to remember what I had eaten for breakfast and to question the health of my spiritual ears.

"YOU WILL GET A POODLE IN CHARLESTON!"

How could it be the Holy Spirit for it seemed totally irrational and somewhat far out? I chose to keep the entire thing under wrap and not tell a single soul, especially my husband! We lived a few blocks from the mental ward of the local hospital and I had no intention of being admitted...!

The weekend finally arrived and we left for Charleston. I should have been overjoyed to finally spend a few days with my husband but I kept on seeing imaginary yappy and hyperactive poodles dancing before my eyes!

Don and I decided, the next morning, to have breakfast on the Isle of Palms and as we waited for our number to be called, I sat next to a southern gentleman, dressed in an extraordinary sorbet color outfit... I could not help but stare at the orange, yappy and hyperactive poodle, which of course, was seated on his lap! I could not help but say a silent prayer to the heavens above,

"Lord, do not let it be this dog!"

Strangely and mysteriously enough, I kept on seeing real yappy and hyperactive poodles wherever I went but I chose not to let these critters rob me of shopping on King Street, visiting lovely art galleries and discovering old plantations.

As we drove back late on Sunday evening, my husband and I kept on reminiscing over the past two days and somehow, somewhere, my feelings got hurt by one of his comments and I chose silence as a way to pay him back! I turned to the right and decided to stare at the night, dark fleeting shadows and a ghostly and unfamiliar landscape.

We were now a long way from Charleston and yet, still in South Carolina. I have never forgotten what happened next for my husband's words are still permanently engraved in my memory. As I turned around to stare at his profile, I can still see him and hear him pray as if it were yesterday.

"Lord, Daniele has had a really rough year. Would You please give her a male apricot poodle...!"

My heart stopped for I had not told a single soul and I was still far from being convinced that what I had heard, came from the heavens above!

As I sat at my computer desk, on the next morning, I typed in three words... "male apricot poodle"! Out of nowhere, the picture of the most exquisite little apricot male poodle came up on my screen instead of a long list of potential breeders.

I have tried, to this day, to replicate what had just happened but have never been able to do so.

Out of curiosity, I decided to call the number listed at the bottom of the screen and discovered that the dog's owner lived less than ten miles from my husband's office!

I could no longer keep quiet and informed him that his prayers had already been answered.

By the end of the day, we were the proud owners of a high-spirited tiny male apricot poodle puppy and our zoo was enlarged by one more critter. It still did not make any sense but we had learned, over the years, to go with God's flow.

The answer came exactly two months later when I was diagnosed with cancer.

God had known all along that I would need this creamy apricot fur ball to keep me going and make me laugh in the midst of surgeries and treatments.

God had known that I would need a little companion who would faithfully follow me wherever I went and would jump on my lap every time I sat or lay down.

God had known that I would need another dog for

our beloved Great Pyrenees, Chloe, died of cancer a few days before I faced an array of tests and surgical procedures.

Every time I looked at his adoring brown eyes, I could almost see the face of God

Every time I heard him yap around the house, I was reminded of the promise God had given me before we had left for Charleston.

Being forewarned that I would get a poodle in Charleston, listening to the prayers of my husband asking for such a dog and finding one, a few short miles from our house, was nothing short than miraculous and a reminder of His extraordinary and extravagant love!

God chooses, at times, to appear irrational and thus, confound the wise!

He not always gives us what we want but He often gives us what we need!

I did not want a third dog but He knew that I was about to need one. Cancer was waiting in the aisle of my life and our beloved Great Pyrenees would be gone in less than two months!

He is and has always been the author of perfect gifts sent from above at the perfect time.

We are loved and God will shake heaven and earth

together to give us a male apricot poodle puppy if He knows we will need one at some time in the future.

But I wish He did something about the yapping...!

THIRTY-NINE

A mortal enemy

I had not felt like myself for a few months but could not really figure out why!

In the deepest core of my being, I knew that something was not right but for the time being, I was neither willing nor able to face and expose this new threat to my life and my happiness.

Doctors did not seem to find anything wrong and as always, had attributed my symptoms to my age and my fluctuating hormones but as a precautionary measure, had recommended a routine mammogram!

As I stood, half-naked and very vulnerable before an x-ray machine, I had an uncanny sense of foreboding! I somehow knew that I was about to step into an unfamiliar battlefield and confront new and powerful enemies...

For some strange and unethical reasons, my family practitioner never gave me the results of the mammogram! But a kind technician called me at home and strongly encouraged me to get a second test, as soon as possible. I knew at that moment that

I had cancer and we rapidly left for Duke Medical Center where, once again, I would place my life into the hands of skilled and knowledgeable doctors and surgeons.

But above all, I also chose to place my cancer into the hands of the One who, long ago, had formed me and loved me.

Little did I know that He was about to show Himself bigger and more powerful that I had ever imagined Him or known Him to be?

Little did I know that Don was about to show himself strong, loving and supportive, as I had always wanted him to be?

Little did I know that my inner strength, my faith and my determination were about to be challenged and shaken to their cores?

Each passage of scripture that I had ever read, studied or taught would be tested by fire.

Each prayer that I had ever prayed would be challenged.

My emotions and my fears were now in full control, creating havoc and preventing me from thinking clearly and rationally.

I knew that my life was in danger and I DID NOT want to die!

Maybe later but certainly, NOT NOW!

As I approached a long series of medical tests to determine the exact location of the cancer, I could not help but be afraid and yet, I still vividly remembered the words that I had said so many times,

"Fear and faith cannot cohabit in your heart! One has to go!"

How do you chase away fear in the midst of a life and death situation?

How do you chase away what is now paralyzing you?

How do you chase away an enemy, which is far greater and far more dangerous than cancer itself?

"Although I walk through the valley of the shadow of death, I will fear no evil for thou art with me..."

I was on the threshold of a new journey but I did not want to walk its path alone.

I was weak and fearful and the only words that I could recite, at that moment, were the Lord's Prayer.

My trust was not in my faith, for it was long gone.

My trust was in the words that I had loved and cherished throughout my entire life.

My trust was in my Father, who was in heaven and whose will would ultimately be done in my life, my destiny and my body.

As predicted, I crossed many dark and fearful valleys, but not once did He abandon me. I had been given an extra dose of supernatural joy which carried me through and which often, I had to tone down, when I found myself in the midst of other deadly ill cancer patients.

My intentions were not to show off or embarrass other people, and I would often ask Don, as we were about to enter crowded waiting rooms,

Am I showing "it" too much? Should I tone "it" down?

Whether I made it or not, still mattered but in the midst of my "one on one" with death and life, I had chosen to proclaim His goodness in the hallways of Duke Hospital. I had chosen to let my heart escape and dance to the sound of a heavenly choir!

Had I not said during one of my past teachings,

"If you are willing, God will give you a chance to dance…"

This new and totally unexpected joy became my life force and never left me throughout the course of my cancer and the treatments my doctors chose to have me go through.

I had no need to fear evil for not once, did I feel alone and not once, did God leave my side!

I still remember, one occasion, in particular, which demonstrated His willingness to be with me, in the midst of a very painful procedure that I was forced to go through. The doctors wanted to find out if the cancer cells had spread to my lymph nodes.

They also needed to know the exact location of my cancer so as not to miss anything during my upcoming surgery.

I had been scheduled for a "sentinel node" nuclear test and as I lay on a cold and icy table, I had been forewarned that the procedure would actually be very painful. I would no longer be talking about a mere "one to ten" pain level for I was about to hit the stratosphere without the help of much needed drugs! I was about to be injected with a radioactive marker, which, being a doctor's wife, I knew would feel like acid burning my flesh and my bones!

I was told to be strong but how could I be? I was petrified!

As the physician was getting ready to inject my breast with this much dreaded radioactive marker, I ordered him to stop and give me ten minutes to gather my thoughts, calm my emotions and start deep and slow breathing!

My goal was to be in such a meditative state that I would HOPEFULLY be able to withstand this medical procedure!

But above all, I asked the Holy Spirit to be with me and not let me down...!

He did not, for in the midst of my deep breathing, I heard Him say,

"No matter what, DO NOT open your eyes!"

Being as claustrophobic as I am, I would not have survived if indeed I had opened my eyes for I soon realized that the technicians had locked me into a very tight and very small box while the needle was slowly and carefully being guided into the tumor!

But I was not alone in that box and with the added help of my deep breathing and meditative state, I was soon able to tell the doctor to go ahead and politely order the nurse to let go of my hand for as much as she wanted to help me, she was not!

I felt everything but remarkably and miraculously enough it did not hurt!

Fear had tried and would try time after time to bring me down in the midst of my cancer journey, but joy was and stayed my invisible force, my strength and my shield!

I still did not know what the final outcome of my illness would be and whether I would live or not but for the time being, I was cherishing Don's patient, strong and loving support, the prayers of my family and friends and the amazing closeness of a God who had chosen to walk in the midst of my dark valleys.

In the midst of cancer, life was good!

In the midst of cancer, my heart was dancing.

In the midst of cancer, I was continuing to come into being!

FORTY

Thank You, Thank You, Thank You

From the depth of my soul, did I cry to my Creator, as I was about to face surgery.

How could I know His peace and yet, be so afraid?

I felt like a bystander watching a battle being fought between my heart and my emotions.

On one hand, I knew that God was watching over me and would continue walking with me through the dark valley I was crossing.

On the other hand, I was very afraid for I knew that this surgery was only the beginning of a long and tenuous journey.

And yet, from the depth of my soul, did I start repeating, over and over again,

Thank You, Thank You, Thank You!"

Not only at that moment but also in the weeks and the months to come. I simply could not stop saying,

Thank you, Thank You, Thank You!"

Fear might still be trying at times to grab me and hold me captive but faith was rising like an eagle across the sky.

I was being carried to a place where I would no longer need to dread the outcome of my surgery and the certainty of weeks of chemo or radiation.

I was being carried to my Creator where I would find protection and serenity in the midst of the gigantic storm I was facing.

These simple words, which had been given to me from high above the clouds, were my constant and daily doses of encouragement.

Throughout my recovery from surgery, I kept on saying, "Thank You."

Throughout my seven weeks of radiation, I kept on repeating, "Thank You."

Throughout my slow return to a near normal life, I kept on shouting, "Thank You!"

Whether I lived or die, my soul had made the decision to say "Thank You."

It could no longer be silent for I had chosen to place my life, my destiny, my body and my cancer into His hands!

And so, like a song, like a prayer, rising from the depth of my soul, I kept on saying,

"Thank You, Thank You, Thank you..."

My words enabled me to soar in the midst of the storm I was facing, high above the clouds.

My prayers enabled me to reach the heavens, fly on eagle's wings and find there the comfort, the strength and the courage that I needed to receive, not only for the moment but also for the days and months to come.

Thank you, Thank You, Thank You.

Thank you, Thank You, Thank You..

Thank you, Thank You, Thank You...

FORTY-ONE

The Eagle

From the depth of my soul, a vision or a dream arose which, to this day, is still ingrained in my memory.

Not only did it give me strength before starting seven gruesome weeks of radiation therapy but much later, it also gave me the courage to write this book.

Was it a dream or a vision?

The answer is not that important and I will leave it up to you to decide.

Whether awake or asleep, I found myself, one night, standing in the courtyard of a beautiful French or Italian villa where every paved stone seemed to have become an exquisite reflection of the sun setting on the horizon.

Trees were bare and covered with golden frost.

No one was there and I felt as if I were trespassing.

Everything was very quiet.

Doors and shutters were closed.

I was so cold.

As I turned to look around, I observed a beautiful cypress tree standing tall and majestic in the corner of the courtyard.

Perched halfway up was an eagle nest.

Sitting inside the nest were an eagle and a small white eaglet.

Not wanting to disturb them, I chose to turn away and stand, alone, in the middle of the courtyard.

I heard, a few seconds later, the sound of a rushing wind and without even looking, I knew that the eagle had left its nest.

I stood, a few seconds later, somewhat frightened for the eagle had chosen to land next to me, at my right side.

Little had I realized how tall he was for he reached up to my shoulders.

Afraid and uncertain, I took a few steps to the left and so did he!

Not knowing what to do next, I stopped and so did he!

"Do not be afraid."

Although not a single word had been spoken between us, I could hear and understand him.

"Do not be afraid. Touch me and you will receive strength from me."

So I began to run my fingers through his feathers and as I did, his warmth and his calmness penetrated the depth of my soul.

There we were, the two of us, alone in a French or Italian villa, at the end of a cold winter afternoon.

This mysterious messenger from the heavens above had chosen to give his strength away that I might be renewed and like him, soar high above the clouds.

He was the force that carried me through in the weeks and months to come.

From the depth of my soul I kept on saying,

"Thank You, Thank You, Thank You..."

From the depth of my soul, I kept on praying,

"Thank You, Thank You, Thank You..."

From the depth of my soul, I kept on shouting,

"Thank You, Thank You, Thank You..."

FORTY-TWO

Being a survivor

I may have won the battle against cancer but I was no longer the woman I used to be for I was now known as a cancer survivor! Because of my fiercely independent nature, I resented being pushed against my will into a new social and medical roster of some kind and for a while I stopped saying that I had had cancer!

I may have won the battle but God was the one who had been fighting in the trenches on my behalf. God was the one who deserved to be applauded and praised! I refused to have an illness define me and for a while, I stopped saying that I had had cancer! I was still as private as I had ever been and wanted to stay that way. This is in no way a condemnation of the many brave people who are proud to call themselves "cancer survivors." Like them, I had overcome a potentially terminal illness but unlike them, I wanted to keep it quiet and private!

I was alive but I was no longer the woman I used to be for most of my physical strength had been wiped out by seven long weeks of radiation treatments.

I was alive but I was learning to take one very short day at a time instead of two or three as I used to do.

What now...?

Not knowing what my medical future would hold, my husband and I decided to leave the small and charming southern town where we had lived for almost five years and move closer to our children and grandchildren.

As I said, it was and still is a small and charming southern town but it was there that I had survived a strong arm robbery, faced a young hoodlum holding a silver handgun, had a large rock thrown at my head through our car's windshield and seen our beloved Pyrenees dog almost poisoned to death at the hand of a careless veterinarian!

I honestly think it was time to go...!

We had both survived a host of exotic and local dramas, which, in some supernatural and mysterious ways, God had used to make us stronger, circumcise our hearts and continue to chip away what was still ours and needed to become His!

Nothing is ever wasted in God's economy, in God's kingdom!

In spite of it all, we had both fallen in love with this small and charming southern town and the many friends who had been my life support during cancer!

Thank you!

Throughout the course of my illness, Don's help had been remarkable and I would not have made it without him for he watched over my medical care and my safety as if he were a hawk! I saw him arguing fearlessly with various doctors, as everyone seemed to scramble trying to choose the safest possible course of action and treatments. Not once did I feel alone for not only did I have my husband but I knew also that I was watched over and protected by the hosts of heaven!

We decided to move to Columbia, South Carolina so as to be closer to our children, grandchildren and a large medical center, just in case…!

I was not looking forward to leaving behind my beloved mountain house, which had been the love of my life for the past twelve years. I have never been very good at saying goodbye and the thought of having to say these words filled my heart with a level of grief that I had not known since leaving the French Alps. As expected, my heart broke on the day we left and I fell to the ground sobbing, knowing that, although we may come back and visit at various times, things would never be the same!

Things are indeed no longer as they used to be! My beautiful garden looks abandoned for no one is there to care for it. Our "Boudchou," as we called our mountain house, has lost its soul for the time being… Bears, wild turkeys and coyotes are back cruising the land and the surrounding woods.

Will I ever again live in this land of enchantment?

A small part of me refuses to stop dreaming...

But for the time being, I was alive and feeling safe, living close to a large medical center and enjoying the nearby presence of my children and grandchildren.

As expected, my husband had, in no time, one of the largest neurology practices in the Southeast for his Yale, Harvard and Duke fame seemed to not only precede him but also follow him wherever he chose to practice medicine! He was as busy as ever, solving complex medical cases, praying with his patients and being the best at what he does!

I was alive but I knew no one! Everything I touched seemed to turn to dust, every door I tried to open slammed in my face and every wall I faced refused to come down... As I cried, with tears running down my face, I kept on repeating the name of Jesus over and over, but without much relief for it felt as if the heavens no longer knew my name! It felt as if I had finally entered the dark night of the soul...!

Little did I know, at the time, that many people get depressed after finishing various cancer treatments for it usually takes a while for the body to adjust and quiet down...!

For the first time in my life, I felt utterly depressed, sad, lonely and yet, strangely enough, unable to receive help from my new "ex-oncologist" who curiously enough, seemed to think that I would get better with time...

Going to Urgent Care might have been a better idea...!

I was alive but I was now living in a very large and still somewhat unsafe southern metropolis where I no longer had a support system, and where my children and grandchildren led very busy lives, filled with school and social activities!

But I was now near a large medical center, just in case!

My dreams of retiring in our mountain house had evaporated into thin air...

Our dreams of forming a healing center in the mountains had also vanished...

Our marriage went through some serious rocky times and there were many days, I was not even sure if we were going to make it as a couple.

Too much had happened in the past few years and although my husband had been amazing and ever so faithful during cancer, he was now back loving medicine and his patients and then, loving me. I felt, once again, as if I were unimportant!

I wanted out for I was tired of having spent a lifetime being alone...

I left, soon after, for the beach where one of my daughters had a summerhouse. I was now living near the beautiful city of Charleston, but, once again, I was alone...!

I no longer had the strength to understand it all but as always, someone did.

I no longer had the desire to fix my marriage but as always, someone did!

I no longer had the need to figure it all out but as always, someone did!

I may have felt as if He no longer knew me by name but He did! For although I was now suffering from a post-cancer depression, I knew in my heart, that He was there, loving me more than ever. He had not forgotten about me and as God had done countless times, He was more determined than ever to see His purpose and His destiny for my life being fulfilled, whether I was depressed or not!

My dreams may have died but they needed to do so, in order that His dream for my life might come to life, might be revealed, might burst forth like a bright morning star in the midst of my darkness. Little did I know, at the time, that His dream for my life would be the product of all my yesterdays?

As I stood on the beach, one morning, staring at a vast ocean, covered with millions of golden, pink and silver prisms, reflecting the early sunrise light, I found myself, once again, in the cathedral of His glory.

Depressed or not, I chose to let my heart worship the creator of such overwhelming beauty.

Depressed or not, I chose to release my life, my marriage, my depression and a host of other things into His hands for He alone, could and would save it all!

Depressed or not, tired or not, I knew that His strength would, once again, be mine if I dared to let my faith soar beyond the horizon, across the clouds and all the way to the heavens.

Cancer had changed me but it had not stolen my true identity. It had made me stronger and more determined than ever to fulfill my ordained days here on earth.

I may not have liked being called a "survivor" but let's be honest, I was and had always been one throughout my life...!

FORTY-THREE

No light to be found

Why do I no longer see your light?
Why do I no longer hear your voice?
It is not as if I had never seen it before.
It is not as if I had never heard it before.
And yet, in the midst of my darkness,
I keep on searching,
I keep on seeking.
I look up to the skies but to no avail,
But there is no light to be found.
And yet, I refuse to lose hope
I keep on waiting,
Only to find utter darkness,
Utter silence and utter stillness.
For there is no light to be found,
There is no voice to be heard.
As you are silent, so I am now silent.
I stumble and fall.
But I no longer ask for help,
For there is no hand to hold on to,
There is no comfort to be found.
Time after time, doors have slammed in
my face.

Time after time, walls have refused to come down.

Many schemes did I devise.
Many endeavors did I embark upon.
And yet, they have all failed.
Many times did I look up to the heavens above,
But there was no light to be found.
Many times did I try to bend my ears,
But there was no voice to be heard.
And so I walked in the midst of utter silence,
Hanging on to past knowledge,
Remembering days of long ago,
Refusing to give up,
Unwilling to forget the love I had known,
Hoping once again to be found.
As I had seen the light coming across a vast sky,
As I had heard a voice piercing through the clouds,
Strong as thunder and soft as a crystal bell,
I dare once again to hope for better days.
Will your voice appease my now anxious heart?
Will your hand sustain me and keep me safe?
Will I then find my way?

But darkness is now enfolding me
And silence has now become my grave.
I am alone and yet I refuse to lose hope.
For in the midst of my darkness, I begin to
see you.
In the midst of my silence, I begin to
hear you.
Not as I had seen you before,
Not as I had heard you before.
It would have been so easy to miss you,
For your light was at first ever so faint.
It would have been so easy not to
hear you,
For your voice was nothing more than a
whisper.
But silence has now become my ally,
And stillness is now my friend.
I see your light shining upon my darkness.
I see your hand reaching across the
clouds to help me walk again.
Your voice is now my traveling companion,
And your love is healing my brokenness.
It was then that I began to see better days,
It was then that I found my way.
For there was a light to be found.
There was a voice to be heard!

FORTY-FOUR

Summer of 2014

One year almost to the day has gone by since I heard the Holy Spirit telling me, or should I say, ordering me to leave my daughter's beach house where I had spent a few months. I was pretty much ordered to leave town, return to Columbia and stay there the entire summer!

This made very little sense and was actually contrary to my husband's orders who himself, had advised me to spend time at the seashore, walk on the beach as much as possible and hopefully by breathing salt air recover from a very severe bronchitis.

Being told that I would have to spend an entire summer in the allergy Mecca of the United States made indeed very little sense other than it had been an order coming from high above!

Was it God's idea of a joke?

Probably not...

So I packed my bags, left my daughter's beach house to go back to a city, which is known to be not only the hottest place on earth but also the allergy capital of the country! I doubt very much that this is true but people, since the beginning of time, seem to have always found a great pleasure in exaggerating facts...!

I had known for a long time that I had been supposed to write a book but had always been afraid to do so for after all, English was not my native language. I had also disliked being pestered by everybody, including my own family, friends and acquaintances and I had no intention to write another sappy grandmother book!

I actually had no intention of writing anything at all but God knew that I would have to receive an order from high above to sit at my computer desk, in June of 2014, and test the waters.

I wish I could tell you that my faith was strong and stoic but it was not!

I wish I could tell you that I was happy being back in my large house and being alone but I was not! For it often felt more like a prison than anything else. I missed my old friends from the little town where we had spent five adventurous years and I missed being one hour away from my beloved mountains.

I was also afraid to open the door to my past and relive my entire life! I was not sure I would have the energy to do so for I had barely recovered from cancer and I was being asked to climb a very high mountain in my old age...!

But I knew better than to say no to an order coming from high above.

So I sat, uncertain and somewhat afraid, at my computer desk and began to see God, on a daily basis, fill my head and my heart with words that I did not even know or had forgotten long ago.

So I sat, uncertain and somewhat afraid, knowing full well that my obedience and my willingness to spend the summer in Columbia would be severely tested in the weeks and months to come.

So I sat, uncertain and somewhat afraid, yet fully convinced in my heart, that God would, as He had done before, show Himself to be my helper. However, I honestly saw this book as nothing but trouble with a capital T! I also knew that I had no choice but to write my story for the time seemed to have been set aside from long ago.

I was alone in a big air-conditioned house and I had no choice but to start writing and keep on writing until the book would be finished.

The time was June 2014 and it was then and there that I began to take an honest look at my past and see my entire life from His perspective and no longer mine. It may have been a journey when I started but it soon became a spiritual pilgrimage, which for the next year would take me far and wide across the two continents I had traversed and the vast ocean I had crossed long ago.

The time that I spent in front of a computer screen became my hermitage of choice.

As God began to show me how He had been on my side, from the time of my birth, I could not help but to trust Him to be my inspiration, my editor and my guardian for the warfare, on the home front, intensified to a level that I had never experienced before.

Would I have started if I had known that writing this book would push aside my normal daily activities and force me to work for hours and days at a time?

Yes! For I had discovered that I loved infinitely more painting with words than brushes. This was one canvas that I was not about to let it be unfinished. I did not need to write this book but I now passionately wanted to...

As days and weeks went by, I could not help but wonder how I could have possibly come up with so many colorful and lyrical images and given an almost magical and unworldly slant to my life tales! But my life had been far from being ordinary and far from being simple and needed to be told in a format of its own!

Writing this book helped me understand how God used absolutely everything that pertained to my past, whether good or bad, to form and mold the person I am now.

I am a product of my yesterdays so as to be prepared for my tomorrows…

I did not have to write this book but in more ways than one, I had to do so.

French people are immensely private and often hard to know. Contrary to my heritage, I have chosen to make my entire life an open book so that people may see God's love, goodness and faithfulness.

It may have been written in the English language but it is still very French in its blunt and often sassy and shocking honesty, in its refusal to be labeled and shoved into a particular religious and denominational group and in its willingness to offer an accurate account of a not so ordinary life!

For I am still a Pentecostal, Evangelical, Protestant and Catholic woman who will keep on refusing to be labeled now and until ages of ages!

I chose to write about His extraordinary faithfulness and His unfathomable power in the face of an often lukewarm, blasé, passive or indifferent church.

I chose to write about God's love in the face of a broken and shattered society and I chose not to give you, the reader, a certain number of steps to fix your own life or to show you how to solve your problems in forty days…!

And yet, my hope is that it will encourage you to embark on a new journey and give you the courage and the audacity to step into living water, go deeper and hold on to the hand of God as if your life depended on it! It actually does...

One year has gone by and Don and I are still together and as much of a team as we have ever been. Like everyone else, we suffered a few tragedies of our own but not once, did we intend to waver from the commitment we had made to God and to each other.

A perfect French ending would have been for Don and I to get a divorce and live happily ever after in the arms of someone else and a few others...!

But we did not!

Another ending would have been to see us retire and live, within the safe confinements of a gated community...! But we did not for we'll both keep on being dreamers until our last breath!

Another ending would have been to move to the mountains and start an Alpha-1 center and this may still happen in God's perfect timing.

As we both wait, trying to figure out what God would have us do in our winter years, our lives are nevertheless full, for we love being near our children and grandchildren.

A small portion of my heart will always be in the mountains but I have learned, over time, to be satisfied and content where God has placed me for the time being even if it is the allergy capital of the United States!

We do not know what the future holds for our lives but for the time being, I am back tending to my rose garden, feeding multiple birds and a few stray cats.

I am alive and well!

Would I have started to write this book if I had started to teach and preach when we first moved to Columbia?

Probably not! For I soon would have been too busy to find the time and the space to write. I needed to be utterly alone and utterly silent to be able to hear a gentle voice coming from across the clouds.

Would I have been able to write objectively if I had been dancing on the mountaintops?

Probably not! For I needed to be in a place where I would have to trust God to give me the patience and the endurance to keep on going, one day at a time, one word at a time, one chapter at a time, for I knew full well that I would not have been able to do it on my own.

The book is now finished and it is no longer mine but in some mysterious ways, it never was!

It has never been about my life and about me but it has always been about God, His goodness, His faithfulness and His love.

Much remains to be known.

Much remains to be understood.

Much remains to be discovered, but I have all the time in the world and I have the rest of eternity to comprehend it all.

Now and ever, and unto ages of ages...!

FORTY-FIVE

The Dream

DO NOT give up! DO NOT give up!
Take your dream out.
DO NOT try to put it back together.
Lay it at My feet.
I alone can put it back together.
DO NOT lay your dream down.
For if you do, I do not have anybody else to pick
it up.
High from above the clouds, I have called you.
Your destiny is to trust Me,
To pick up My dream.

Many have I called,
Many have I spoken to,
Many have I shown the dream to.

They rejected it for the dream was too small,
Not to their liking,
Not fitting their theology.
Little did they know that in rejecting My dream,
They were rejecting Me.

To you, I have given what they would not take.
DO NOT try to understand.

DO NOT try to figure out all things.
You cannot.
It is My dream,
And I alone know how it will be birthed
into reality.

I long to hear you say,
"Here I am, send me."
Then I will be Your Helper, Your Provider,
The answer to all your questions and the
solution to all your dilemmas.

From high above the clouds,
My voice will guide you,
My Spirit will show you the way,
Your dream is now a bigger dream
For it springs from My heart to you.

Acknowledgments

It would be impossible to write the names of all the people who have been involved in the creation of this book.

I will always be grateful to the invaluable help and support of my husband who spent countless hours supporting me and encouraging me. I could not have done it without him!

I want to thank Frances May who took over the household and the cares of our animal kingdom while I was busy writing. She spent countless hours praying and interceding not only for this writer but also on behalf of all the people who will be reading "Across The Clouds."

How can I not be grateful for the amazingly talented team at RR Donnelley who dared to believe in me and carried this book to completion with a great deal of expertise, immense kindness and a great team spirit.

I loved working with all of you and thank you for your patience and support when I lost my cool.

Ashley Simoneaux was a model of kindness and patience.

Valene Kitick let her incredible artistic talents loose when she designed my website.

Thank you Donna K. Rhodes for taking a chance on an unknown writer and supporting me as much as you did.

Above all, I want to thank the Holy Spirit for having been my helper, my master editor and my greatest ally. I could not have written this book without Him and I would not have become who I am today without His constant help and guidance.

Thank you, thank you, thank you...

*"Daniele's book is a classic already.
Like the greatest myths, there is a hero with almost supernatural powers who goes through the dark night of the soul to triumph and find the light. It contains iconic archetypes such as the hero, scientist, patriarch, and jester. The story is told with a dry European wit that keeps us amused and engaged. Each word is carefully chosen for maximum effect like a poem from one of the great masters.*

*Comparable authors come to mind such as:
Alice Walker - The Color Purple
Elizabeth Gilbert - Eat, Pray, Love
Maya Angelou - I Know Why the Caged Bird Sings*

"Across The Clouds" speaks directly to our souls and reminds us of our own hero's saga. We do not grow and stretch and learn when things go right. Pain is our greatest teacher if we only listen. Daniele's book teaches us to be still and listen for the quiet soft voice of God.

Everyone who touches the story will benefit. I cannot wait to see how it unfolds and takes on a life of its own.

Thanks for including us on the ride."

*-Donna K. Rhodes
RR Donnelley*